The Boys and Girls Learn Differently Action Guide for Teachers

PREVIOUS BOOKS BY MICHAEL GURIAN

In Education

Boys and Girls Learn Differently!
(with Patricia Henley and Terry Trueman)

In Parenting

The Soul of the Child
The Wonder of Girls
The Wonder of Boys
A Fine Young Man
The Good Son
What Stories Does My Son Need?
(with Terry Trueman)

In Psychology

Love's Journey
Mothers, Sons and Lovers
The Prince and the King

For Young Adults

Understanding Guys
From Boys to Men

Fiction and Poetry

An American Mystic
The Odyssey of Telemachus
As the Swans Gather

The
Boys and Girls
Learn
Differently

ACTION GUIDE FOR TEACHERS

Michael Gurian

and

Arlette C. Ballew

JOSSEY-BASS
A Wiley Imprint
www.josseybass.com

Published by Jossey-Bass
A Wiley Imprint
989 Market Street, San Francisco, CA 94103-1741   www.josseybass.com

Jossey-Bass books and products are available through most bookstores. To contact Jossey-Bass
directly call our Customer Care Department within the U.S. at 800-956-7739, outside the U.S. at
317-572-3986, or fax 317-572-4002.

Jossey-Bass also publishes its books in a variety of electronic formats. Some content that appears
in print may not be available in electronic books.

Library of Congress Cataloging-in-Publication Data
  Gurian, Michael.
    The boys and girls learn differently action guide for teachers / by Michael Gurian,
Arlette C. Ballew.—1st ed.
      p. cm.
    ISBN 0-7879-6485-9 (alk. paper)
    1. Sex differences in education. 2. Learning, Psychology of. I. Ballew, Arlette C., date. II. Title.
LC212.9 .G87 2004
306.43'2—dc21

                                                                    2002152142

Printed in the United States of America
FIRST EDITION
PB Printing   10 9 8 7 6 5

CONTENTS

9 STRUCTURAL INNOVATIONS — 165

xiv Contents

ACKNOWLEDGMENTS

The authors gratefully acknowledge the editing, production, and marketing staff members at Jossey-Bass, particularly Amy Scott, Alan Rinzler, Seth Schwartz, Lasell Whipple, and Erin Jow.

We want to recognize Patricia Henley and Terry Trueman, who helped to make *Boys and Girls Learn Differently!* a reality, as well as Laurie Allen, Ruben and Raquel Gur, Camilla Benbow, and others who have done laboratory and field research in neurobiology.

Special thanks go to the teachers and other educators who supplied insights, techniques, and activities for *Boys and Girls Learn Differently!* (many of whom are noted in this guide).

Finally, we want to acknowledge and thank the teachers and students who have supplied new insights, techniques, and activities for this publication:

- Chris Christopher, who teaches eleventh- and twelfth-grade trigonometry and strategies (senior math) at Randolph High School in Randolph, Massachusetts.
- Lilly Figueroa, a math and ESL teacher at Broughal Middle School in Bethlehem, Pennsylvania.
- Paul Kaplan, who teaches tenth-grade history at Randolph High School.
- Monica Miller, who teaches kindergarten and first grade at the Thomas H. Benton Elementary School in Columbia, Missouri.

- Stacy Moyer, who teaches first graders who are learning English as their second language at Alexander D. Goode Elementary, York (Pennsylvania) City Schools.
- Janet Rodgers, who is in transition from a career as a public school teacher to a position in higher education. She is completing a Ph.D. in education at the University of Pittsburgh and supervising student teachers for Shippensburg University in Pennsylvania.
- Rita Rome, who teaches art at Memorial Elementary School in Montvale, New Jersey.
- Alissa Sheehan, an eleventh-grade student who conducted a survey of eleventh- and twelfth-grade students at Randolph High School.
- Mary Jo Westwood, Mary Rook, and Jeri Deming, of the Columbia, Missouri, Public Schools, who recommended teachers to us.

The Boys and Girls Learn Differently
Action Guide for Teachers

Schools and educators in the United States are struggling to teach all that they need to teach, maintain discipline, build character, and provide for the safety of the children in their care. They often have to deal with children who are not receiving the emotional, nutritional, and physical care they need; parents who are "too busy" to attend to their children's school issues; pressure from legislators to raise test scores; lack of funding; and lack of parental support. More and more decisions about education are made by politicians, rather than educators, and few policy makers understand the differences between how boys' and girls' brains work, how they differ, and what they need in order to learn.

Applying Brain-Based Research

Teachers who understand brain- and gender-based research (differences in anatomical structure, neurological development, and the chemical and hormonal climate in growing boys and girls) can help to ensure that the children in their care have a chance to find the attachment and bonding they need in order to learn and behave in the ways that are natural to them. This not only optimizes each child's natural learning abilities but also helps to reduce the number of children who are labeled as discipline problems, slow learners, and attention-deficient.

Knowledge of research in brain-based gender differences in how children learn is one of the best tools a teacher can have. In the "ultimate classroom," teachers' efforts are supported by administrators and parents, who are trained in and committed to gender-based education. But teachers can start now to apply what they have learned in their own classrooms, while urging greater changes at the school, school district, and state levels. This guide was developed to help teachers create and adapt techniques, activities, games, rituals, and other learning innovations that use knowledge of how boys and girls brains work and what they need at different stages of school life. With time and effort, we can institute gender-appropriate educational techniques that bring the greatest benefit to all our children.

Boys and Girls Learn Differently!

This guide and *Boys and Girls Learn Differently!*—on which it is based—incorporate over twenty-five years of research pertaining to differences in the behaviors and learning styles of male and female schoolchildren. *Boys and Girls Learn Differently!* explains

- Neurological and endocrinological (hormonal) effects on learning and behavior
- Developmental psychology, especially the effects of natural human developmental cycles on learning and behavior
- Gender research on neurobiological and environmental differences (and similarities) between boys and girls

The biological and neurological information in *Boys and Girls Learn Differently!* comes from sources listed in the Notes and the Additional Resources of that book. Michael Gurian also studied thirty cultures to make sure that the conclusions presented in the book had worldwide validity. The book explains areas in which boys and girls are weak and strong, vulnerable and dominant, and tells how teachers and parents can apply the knowledge to classrooms and other child-learning environments.

Using This Guide

To provide a background for planning brain- and gender-based classroom activities, techniques, and other innovations, the research described in *Boys and Girls Learn Differently!* is summarized in this guide, and many of the classroom activities, techniques, and structural innovations offered by teachers and other educational specialists trained by the Gurian Institute are included.

In addition, this guide contains pertinent new background material; many new classroom techniques, activities, and other innovations used by teachers and school systems; and new, useful resources.

We hope that you will find ways to adapt these techniques and activities and create new ones suited to your own students, subjects, grade levels, and special needs. The goal of such innovations is to create the "ultimate classroom" in all grades from preschool through high school.

This guide also is structured differently from *Boys and Girls Learn Differently!* Many chapters are devoted to specific areas of learning, and grades from preschool through high school are discussed within those chapters, as appropriate.

Teachers will find that most of the background information and many of the techniques, activities, and other innovations appropriate to one grade level can be applied, at least in part, to other grades. Similarly, insights and innovations from one topical heading can be used by teachers who are primarily interested in other topical headings. Therefore, we urge you to read all sections rather than focusing only on the ones that, at first glance, may seem most pertinent to your classroom(s).

This guide also contains a new discussion of experiential learning—a way of helping children "learn how to learn"—and a format for designing new classroom activities, games, and educational innovations based on the research.

We hope that, as you work your way through this publication, you will find practical assistance in your efforts to better help the children in your care to learn and thrive. The ultimate classroom best fits the nature of each individual child. It involves changes in school and classroom structures, functions, and emotive opportunities, how senses and physical activity are used, and how parents are advised to help their children learn. We hope that you will find countless ways to create the ultimate classroom in your school.

The Contents of This Guide

Chapter One, "Background: How the Brain Learns," describes inherent differences between boys' and girls' brains; the reasons for these differences; and how the differences are manifest in boys and girls in terms of learning styles and various types of intelligences. It also describes how brain-based gender research indicates the need for change in our schools, in nine critical areas.

Chapter Two, "Bonding and Attachment," explains the vital role of bonding and attachment in a child's behavioral, psychological, and intellectual growth. It describes sources of, and techniques for dealing with, children's emotional stress; the importance of mentors, community involvement, and rites of passage in a child's life; and tips regarding communication and conflict resolution that maintain teacher-student bonds.

This chapter and each of the succeeding chapters is divided into sections devoted to preschool and kindergarten, elementary school, middle school, and high school. Each section presents successful techniques and activities that teachers and school systems actually use, and many of these are applicable to other grade levels as well.

Chapter Three, "Discipline and Related Issues," includes a discussion of aggression and its role in development (especially male development). It offers insights into how to deal with aggression in young children through empathy nurturance and verbalization and how to teach conflict management and anger management to older students. It presents the reasons for many disciplinary problems (including the effect of the media on student behavior), techniques for motivating all students and preventing disciplinary problems, and successful disciplinary strategies and techniques used by educators at all grade levels. In addition, it discusses the need for schools to deal with harassment and cruelty and to offer character-education programs.

Chapter Four, "Math, Science, and Spatial Learning," explains why boys tend to do better than girls in these areas and what educators can do to help all students learn more easily and effectively. Topics include self-directed activities; use of the physical environment in teaching math and science; and how to make math more "hands-on" with the use of manipulatives, games, and other activities that encourage spatial and logical-mathematical thinking. This chapter also highlights the need to vary teaching media and strategies in order to help girls and nonspatial boys to process math calculations and science data. Special sections on the use of computers make recommendations about computer usage and education at the different school levels, and the importance of encouraging students to learn math, science, and other technologies is reinforced.

This chapter also introduces an important theme, the use of learning pairs and groups; this theme is continued in subsequent chapters.

Chapter Five is "Language, Reading, Writing, and Social Science." As in the other chapters, the use of movement and manipulatives in learning and the need to use multisensory stimulation and a variety of learning modalities in order to teach to children's visual, auditory, and kinesthetic learning modes are discussed. Structural techniques include peer tutoring, cooperative groups, same-sex learning, scholarly discourse, and connecting language arts and history to other experiential processes. This chapter also discusses how to tie language, reading, writing, and social-science classes into character development.

Chapter Six, "Physical Learning and Nutrition," explains why young children, especially boys, need to move around as they learn. It describes the current crisis in the United States from the lack of proper nutrition and the lack of vigorous physical activity that is necessary for full physical, intellectual, and psychosocial development. It presents activities and techniques for developing fine motor skills and using the outdoor classroom. In discussing the proper roles of sports, athletics, and competition in child development, the authors make recommendations for physical activities that should be included in the curriculum for different age levels. They tell how athletics can help cut down on discipline problems among adolescents and also why mixed-gender sports in which teen-aged males and females (who are already undergoing the gender-driven stresses and confusions of adolescence) have to engage in tactile contact are not advisable. Finally, this chapter describes the detrimental effects of obesity in children; explains the effects of carbohydrates, proteins, and omega-3 fatty acids on the developing body and brain; and makes recommendations for the intake of these foods based on the time of day and physical needs.

Special education is discussed in Chapter Seven, which explores why so many students diagnosed as having learning disorders or attention deficits are boys. It also notes the need to pay attention to the special needs of girls, whose disabilities often are not as marked as those of boys. Discussions cover the use of psychotropic medications; the special ed student's need for emotional bonds, safety, consistency, and discipline; and the school-home alliance. Activities and innovations that teachers use in their special ed classes are presented, including those that highlight the use of movement, a multisensory approach, and motivational techniques.

Chapter Eight, "Planning Your Own Experiential Activities," explains the rationale for experiential learning, which is exemplified in most of the techniques and activities described in this guide. It also describes the six stages of the natural learning process and how knowledge of this process can help students "learn how to learn"; the role of the teacher as facilitator; and the types of activities and learning technologies that can be used to encourage lasting learning. Important factors to consider when planning experiential-learning interventions are presented. The chapter concludes with a checklist to use in planning and developing personalized learning experiences and a summary of the developmental themes in this book, categorized by school level.

Chapter Nine makes a case for needed *structural innovations* at all school levels. Structural innovations are included here because gender-specific innovations are easier to implement when major structural innovations are in place. Recommended school-wide innovations include more parent involvement, year-round schooling, change in the timing of the school day, changes in class size and number of teachers, separate-sex education, school uniforms or dress codes, teacher teams, multigenerational mentoring, psychosocial and gender education for adolescents, changes in standardized testing, and an end to grade inflation. Classroom innovations include increased use of learning pairs and learning groups, rite-of-passage experiences, multigenerational learning, breaks from didactic learning, and more experiential learning. As with all chapters, examples of things that teachers and schools are successfully doing to bring these changes about are presented.

The Appendix, "Working with Parents," contains lists of actions that schools and teachers can take to involve parents and community members in the education and welfare of students. This involvement can make or break a school's or a teacher's ability to implement the changes, innovations, and techniques that are mandated by gender- and brain-based research and our knowledge of what we can do to improve and enrich our children's development and learning.

"References and Resources" contains a wealth of information about publications, programs, services, Websites, and organizations that can help teachers to apply what they know about the learning needs of boys and girls in their schools and classrooms.

Background

HOW THE BRAIN LEARNS

THE HUMAN BRAIN HAS ONE HUNDRED BILLION NEURONS AND ONE HUNDRED TRILLION connecting cells. An adult brain is approximately four to eight pounds of dense matter in three major layers: the *cerebral cortex* at the top; the *limbic system* in the middle; and the *brain stem* at the bottom, connecting with the spinal cord. The brain grows from the bottom up, the upper limbic system and the four lobes of the cerebral cortex (neocortex) developing later than the lower limbic system and brain stem.

In general, the three layers of the brain are known for distinct functions, although all functioning areas of the brain constantly interact.

The *brain stem* is where fight-or-flight responses are harbored. This most primitive part of the brain is essential for survival.

The *limbic system* generally is where emotion is processed. A sensory stimulant comes into the brain through the eyes, ears, skin, or other organs, and the person experiences an emotive response to it. Although some aggressive responses are brain-stem responses, others come from the limbic system as well—specifically from the amygdala, which lies at the bottom of the limbic system, just above the brain stem.

The four lobes at the top of the brain are where thinking generally occurs. In each lobe, different sensory stimulants are processed. Certain cortices in the top of the brain (for example, the prefrontal cortex) handle the majority of moral and

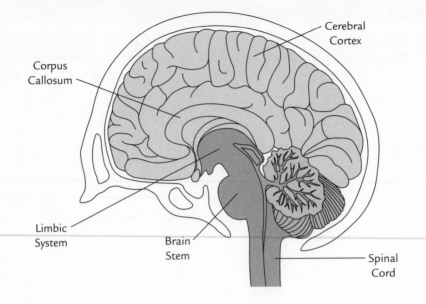

other decision making. The top of the brain is divided into the left and the right hemispheres. The left is primarily associated with verbal skills—speaking, reading, and writing—and the right is primarily associated with spatial skills, such as measuring, perceiving direction, and working with blocks or other objects.

When a child is learning the implications of a novel or how to do math, the top of the brain generally is involved, although emotional responses often occur, especially if the student has an emotional reaction to the content of the lesson. In this way, the neocortex and the limbic system work together. Examples of emotional reactions are "I feel sympathy for Hester Prynne" and "I can't do this; it's too hard." The emotive response in the limbic system can slow down or shut off most thinking in the top of the brain. In neurological terms, a child who thinks she can't do something might fulfill her own thinking; during the crisis of esteem, her blood flow remains heavily in the middle of the brain, not moving up to the thinking centers.

Inherent Differences Between Boys' and Girls' Brains

Researchers, such as Laurie Allen at UCLA, Ruben Gur at the University of Pennsylvania, and Camilla Benbow at the University of Iowa, have discovered structural and functional differences in male and female brains and gender-different approaches to learning and living that result primarily from brain differences, not environmental forces. Their research has been corroborated worldwide.

Boys and Girls Learn Differently! helps teachers become aware of how the brain learns in general and how boys' and girls' brains learn differently. With this understanding, teachers can help children accept their differences and celebrate their natural strengths. They can also aid them in compensating for their natural weaknesses.

Differences between girls and boys are not evidence of gender superiority or inferiority. There are some things boys tend to be better at than girls, and vice versa. Of course, there are exceptions. Brain differences are best understood as a spectrum, rather than as female and male poles. There are also "bridge brained" children, who have nearly equal qualities of male and female characteristics. Their brains are the most "bi-gender."

Developmental and Structural Differences

Most females' brains mature earlier and more quickly than those of males. Brain development in infants is often most pronounced in the right hemisphere and gradually moves to the left. The movement starts earlier in females than in males. Girls may acquire complex verbal skills as much as a year earlier than boys do. Often, a preschool girl reads faster and with a larger vocabulary, and speaks with better grammar, than does a preschool boy.

One of the last steps in the brain's growth occurs as the nerves that spiral around the shaft of other nerves of the brain are coated with myelin, which allows electrical impulses to travel down each nerve quickly and efficiently. An older child is generally more developed than a younger one, in large part because of myelination. Myelination continues in all brains into the early twenties, but is complete in young women earlier than in young men.

The corpus callosum is the bundle of nerves that connects the right and left brain hemispheres. It is up to 20 percent larger in females than in males, giving girls better cross-talk between the hemispheres. There is more (and quicker) development in females than in males in the prefrontal lobes, where regulation of emotion finds its executive decision making, and the occipital lobes, where sensory processing often occurs.

Girls take in more sensory data than boys do. On average, they hear better, smell better, and take in more information through the fingertips and skin. Females tend to be better than males at controlling impulsive behavior. They tend to self-monitor high-risk and immoral conduct better than males—especially if the boys and girls are equally untrained in ethics or impulse control, so girls are less likely to take moral risks than boys. Boys are more likely to show physical aggression.

Girls tend to have better verbal abilities and rely heavily on verbal communication; boys tend to rely heavily on nonverbal communication, being innately less able to verbalize feelings and responses as quickly as girls.

Males tend to have more development in certain areas of the right hemisphere, which provides them with better spatial abilities, such as measuring, mechanical design, geography, and map reading.

Chemical and Hormonal Differences

Males and females have different amounts of most brain chemicals. The male brain secretes less serotonin than the female brain, making males more impulsive and fidgety. The crying of a child stimulates secretion of oxytocin in the female brain to a far greater degree than in the male brain. Oxytocin is one of the brain chemicals that, being more constantly stimulated in females, make the female capable of quick and immediate empathic responses to others' pain and needs.

Males and females possess all human hormones, but females are dominated by estrogen and progesterone, and males are dominated by testosterone. These hormones have contrasting effects. Progesterone is a female growth hormone and the bonding hormone. Female hormonal levels vary with the menstrual cycle and other circumstances (for example, hearing a child cry, seeing another person suffer, being pregnant, competing), making females' moods swing. Testosterone is the male growth hormone and the sex-drive and aggression hormone. Males receive five to seven surges of testosterone every day, beginning in prepuberty (around age ten). During these, hormonal flow can make their moods vacillate between aggressive and withdrawn.

A girl may be likely to bond first and ask questions later. A boy might be aggressive first and ask questions later. A girl is likely to try to manage social bonds in a group situation through egalitarian alliances, but a boy tends to manage social energy by striving for dominance or pecking order.

Scientists long believed that the human reaction to stress was "fight or flight," but most stress research had been done on males. A UCLA study—reported by Taylor, Klein, Lewis, Gruenewald, Gurung, and Updegraff in 2000—suggests that part of a woman's response to stress is oxytocin, which buffers the fight-or-flight response and causes her to tend to children and gather in friendship and collaboration with other women. During these acts, more oxytocin is released, which further counters stress and produces a calming effect. This calming response does not occur in men, because testosterone, which stressed men produce in high levels, seems to reduce the effects of oxytocin. Estrogen seems to enhance it.

Hormones also influence learning ability. For instance, when her estrogen is high, a girl scores higher on both standardized and in-class tests than when it is low. When a boy's testosterone is high, he performs better on spatial exams, such as math tests, but worse on verbal tests.

Hormonal levels vary in both boys and girls. Some boys are high-testosterone (very aggressive, socially ambitious, striving for dominance, heavy in muscle mass). Some boys are low-testosterone (more sensitive, softer in appearance and manner). By adulthood, males can have six to twenty times more testosterone than females. When both males and females compete, their testosterone levels go up, but because males have much higher testosterone, they tend to be more aggressively competitive than females. Females can increase their testosterone by competing more. Women who received testosterone in clinical tests become more independent, socially ambitious, and aggressive.

Functional Differences

Boys use the right hemisphere of the brain more, girls the left. Boys move more emotive material down from the limbic system to the brain stem, where fight-or-flight responses are stored; girls move more of it upward to the upper brain, where complex thought occurs. Ruben Gur has used brain-imaging techniques to show that the resting female brain is as active as the activated male brain. The female brain uses its resources quickly and often and in more places. Therefore, the female brain has a learning advantage.

Quite often a girl's response to a situation is more complex than a boy's. Males tend to manage stimulants with more of what is called "task focus."

Because the male brain is not as activated in as many places, it becomes overwhelmed by stimulation more quickly, causing it to decide on the importance of stimulants for their necessity to a task. A lot goes untouched by the male brain because it does not attend to those things, preferring to manage stimulation by "sticking to a plan." The advantage in this is a quick, direct route to a goal. A disadvantage is that if the task goes badly or failure emerges, the male has fewer resources to redirect himself.

Two areas of greater functioning in the female are memory and sensory intake. Two areas of greater functioning in the male are in spatial tasks and abstract reasoning. Boys have the edge in dealing with spatial relationships (such as objects and theorems); a girl's brain responds more quickly to a greater quantity of sensory information, connecting it with the primacy of personal relationships and communication.

Girls can store, for short periods, a greater quantity of seemingly random information; boys can do this more often if the information is organized into some coherent form or has specific importance to them. Boys can store trivia for a long time better than girls can.

Females react acutely and quickly to pain, but their overall resistance to long-term discomfort is stronger than is males.

There is strong evidence that males and females taste things differently. Generally, females are sensitive to bitter flavors and prefer high concentrations of sweet things. Males are attracted to salty flavors. The female's nose and palate are more sensitive than the male's. Olfactory sensitivity increases in males when they are around females who are about to ovulate.

➡ *Adapting to Hearing Differences:* Because females are able to hear better than males, sometimes a loud voice is needed for boys. This makes an interesting case for keeping boys near the front of the classroom.

➡ *Adapting to Visual Differences:* Males and females see things differently. Females are generally far better at seeing in a darkened room, whereas males see better than females in bright light. This suggests how teachers should arrange their students in terms of distance or closeness to visual learning aids.

Another intriguing difference applies to teaching music and choir. Six times as many girls can sing in tune as boys.

Differences in Processing Emotion

Brain-based research shows us that processing emotion is an area in which boys are more at risk for missed learning and processing opportunities. The female brain processes more emotive stimulants, through more senses, and more completely than does the male. It also verbalizes emotive information quickly.

When sensory information laden with emotive content comes into the female limbic system, brain activity may move quickly into the four lobes at the top of the brain, where thinking occurs. This makes a female more likely to process hurt and talk about it with others, since more of her activity moves up to the hemispheres that verbalize and reason over the crisis. In this way, females are emotionally tougher; they cry or talk about their distress.

In similar conditions, the male brain seems to move information quickly toward the bottom of the limbic system (the amygdala) and the brain stem, so the male is likely to become physically aggressive or withdrawn (fight or flight). The male's response short-circuits intellectual and academic learning because his emotive processing takes longer and involves less reasoning; in addition, less of his emotional crisis–response neural firing is in the top of the brain, where learning is occurring.

Boys can sometimes take hours to process emotively (and manage the same information as girls). This makes males more emotionally fragile than we tend to think they are. A boy who has had a crisis at home may come to school with a higher stress hormone (cortisol) level than his sister because he has held in, not processed, the emotional stress of the crisis. He may be unable to learn for much of the morning, whereas his sister may quickly process and talk out the stress so that she can learn efficiently. The boy often cannot guide his own emotional processing, especially through words.

Girls are fragile in that they often take things personally. Because girls process more emotive information, they may become overwhelmed by the emotional material.

Of course, there are exceptions to this scenario. Many girls become aggressive and shut down after a crisis, and many boys can shut off their emotions and get to work. However, if we see children who are having trouble learning because they do not have the emotive skills to process feelings quickly or in healthy ways, we must intervene to help them move the emotive information upward. This does not just mean "talk it out," because emotionality is only partially about using words.

Why There Are Differences
Between Male and Female Brains

A Brief History of Brain Differences

Until about ten thousand years ago, when the agricultural age arose in many parts of the world, human males were hunters (a very spatial occupation), protectors, and warriors (very aggressive occupations). Females gathered vegetation and cared for children (sensory and verbal occupations). Males built most of the large structures, forming large teams to carry out action. Females did more work inside the structures, arranging and managing home spaces. They worked and verbalized in pairs, triads, and intimate groups.

Females became better at verbal skills; males became better at spatials and more physically aggressive. Females had to care more about small-group consensus; males had to rely more on hierarchies with dominant leadership. Females had to use all their senses and remember variety among things in order to provide child care; males had to focus on single tasks to provide for and protect their communities. Over time, their brains and brain hormones—catalysts for brain activity—came to differ with gender.

The differences exist even in utero (for example, male babies tend to be aggressive, kicking the mother more). Socialization enhances these tendencies in many cultures. In small tribal cultures in which competition for resources within a community is not strong, everyone works together closely, and there are few—if any—wars with other tribes, there are fewer gender differences. In cultures with larger populations where there is great competition for resources, family units are increasingly independent of one another, and conflict with other cultures is a threat, there are more gender differences.

In some ways, boys and girls are becoming more alike (boys are learning to verbalize feelings better, and girls are learning to compete better on athletic and work teams), but they are also becoming more different. More males are born with high testosterone; more females are born with high estrogen and progesterone. Solutions to the problems being experienced in schools involve helping both the more androgynous children and the more gender-different.

Hormones in Utero and at Puberty

All fetuses start out female. In the first trimester of pregnancy, surges of testosterone from the mother's ovaries create the male. One set of surges compels the genitals to drop pelvically and become the penis and testicles. Another wires the brain toward male structure and functioning.

During puberty, when surges of testosterone, estrogen, progesterone, prolactin, and other hormones occur, the brain changes toward increased genderization. In both sexes, surges of testosterone swell the amygdala (the part of the limbic system that generates feelings of fear and anger). This is especially pronounced in boys, which explains the rise in aggressiveness seen in both sexes at adolescence, especially in males, who become high-risk. Increased estrogen at puberty causes sudden growth of the hippocampus, the part of the brain that focuses on memory. The hippocampus in girls grows larger than in boys—one reason that females are better than males at remembering things such as names and faces in social relationships. Hormones change a teenager's sex drive, along with many other attitudes and behaviors, such as irritability, aggressiveness, and moodiness.

Researchers have found that a shift in prenatal hormones can affect us in ways that may not become clear until later in life. Testosterone shapes centers in the brain that process spatial information. In studies of girls with congenital adrenal hyperplasia—a condition that causes the adrenal glands to make excess androgen (a testosterone-like hormone) during prenatal development—their brains were found to be permanently changed. They were more aggressive than their sisters and had better spatial skills (such as the ability to rotate objects in their minds or to imagine how pieces of a puzzle fit together). These girls were also more interested than their sisters in becoming "engineers and pilots."

Hormonal and structural brain differences have profound effects on how males and females learn, act, and live. The following are a few examples.

PRESCHOOL AND KINDERGARTEN Preschool and kindergarten boys and girls often show distinct psychosocial styles, gravitate toward their own gender groups, and often play in their own natural gender roles. For example, little girls use dolls to play at having babies; little boys typically head for the area where the building blocks are. The girls wait more patiently than the boys.

ELEMENTARY SCHOOL Boys and girls become fixed in their gender identities in elementary school, usually by about the fourth grade. Girls typically appear to develop learning abilities with more flexibility and have less trouble than boys do. Ninety percent of elementary school teachers are female, and 99 percent of these have not been trained in how boys and girls learn differently. If structural mistakes in classrooms are being made, girls—learning in a female-oriented environment—can make natural adaptations more easily than boys.

Boys seem to be more impulsive and undisciplined than girls. Reading and writing are hard for a lot of boys. More boys than girls are underachievers, many are unable to focus, and many are diagnosed as having learning disorders.

MIDDLE SCHOOL A middle school-aged child experiences a variety of insights and stresses. There is massive growth of the brain's cognitive and abstract skills in the neocortex. The body experiences puberty, moving with the brain from childhood to adulthood. Boys begin to act and think more like young men, and girls begin to act and think more like young women.

HIGH SCHOOL High school is a time of refinement for all students, in both brain and gender development. In the brain, myelination of cells continues through the early college years. Development in the prefrontal cortex continues at least until college age, with female prefrontal growth moving a little more quickly than male. For the physical or psychological late-maturer, the first two years of high school are developmental years like middle school, and these students are especially tender. For nearly all high school students, the last two years are when intense mentoring in "gender symbiosis" (how females and males can relate in society harmoniously) is required.

How Brain-Based Differences Affect Boys and Girls

Learning-Style Differences

Worldwide brain-based research shows ten areas of difference. Teachers can apply knowledge of these differences in their classrooms, helping both male and female learning styles to flourish.

1. DEDUCTIVE AND INDUCTIVE REASONING Boys tend to be deductive in their conceptualizations, starting their reasoning process from a general principle and applying it, or ancillary principles, to individual cases. They tend to do deductive reasoning more quickly than girls do; this typically has given them an advantage in fast multiple-choice tests, such as SATs.

Girls tend to favor inductive thinking. They tend to begin with specific, concrete examples and then build general theory, adding more and more to their base of conceptualization. It is often easy to teach them concretion, especially in verbalization and writing. Giving an example is often easier for girls to do than boys, especially early in the conceptualization process.

2. ABSTRACT AND CONCRETE REASONING Boys tend to be better than girls at being able to calculate something without seeing or touching it. Boys often do better than girls when mathematics is taught abstractly on a board. The female brain often finds it easier when it is taught using manipulatives and objects (for example, physical number chains).

Males like abstract arguments, philosophical conundrums, and moral debates about abstract principles; in general, the abstract is explored more by the male brain than by the female brain. Architecture and engineering, which rely so much on abstract design principles, are areas toward which the male brain has gravitated. Bridge-brain females often excel in industrial design and their spatial abilities often surpass those of many boys.

3. USE OF LANGUAGE On average, females produce more words than males. During the learning process, girls use more words; boys use fewer words and often work silently. There is more parity in word use in a female group. In a male group, one or two dominant or attention-seeking males may use a lot of words and the other males use far fewer.

Girls tend to prefer to have things conceptualized in everyday language with concrete details. They are not as interested in verbal obfuscation. Boys often find jargon and coded language (for example, from sports, the law, and the military) more interesting and tend to use coded language to communicate.

4. LOGIC AND EVIDENCE Girls are generally better listeners than boys, hear more of what's said, and are more receptive to details in a lesson or conversation. This gives them security in the complex flow of conversation and less need to control conversation with dominance behavior or rules. Girls seem to feel safe with less logical sequencing and more instructional meandering.

Boys tend to hear less and more often ask for clear evidence to support another's claim.

5. THE LIKELIHOOD OF BOREDOM Boys are bored more easily than girls; it often requires more and varying stimuli to keep them attentive. Girls are better at self-managing boredom. This has a profound impact on learning. Once a child has become bored, he is likely to give up on learning and to act out in a way that disrupts the class and causes him to be labeled a behavioral problem.

6. USE OF SPACE Boys tend to need to use more space than girls do when they learn, especially at younger ages. When a girl and a boy are put together at a table, the boy generally spreads his work into the girl's space, not vice versa. This tendency can affect psychosocial dynamics. Teachers may consider the boys impolite or aggressive. In fact, they are often just learning in the way their spatial brains require.

7. MOVEMENT Movement seems to stimulate male brains and helps to manage impulsive behavior. Movement is natural to boys in a closed space, thanks to their lower serotonin and higher metabolism, which create fidgeting behavior. Girls do not generally need to move around as much while learning. The following are some examples of how teachers deal with children's need for movement.

➡ *Giving Boys Something to Touch:* Teachers often find that it helps a boy to play with something (silently), such as a Nerf® ball, while he's learning. He's moving, his brain is being stimulated, he feels comfortable, and no one else is being bothered.

➡ *Giving Boys Chores:* Many teachers find that boys who can't stop moving in class can be managed by putting them to work, for example, letting them hand out papers, sharpen pencils, clean the classroom, help other children with their work, or help the teacher to move things.

➡ *Modeling Clay and Doodling:* Rita Rome, an elementary school art teacher, deals with students' needs to fidget by having modeling clay available so that students can keep their hands busy while they look at her. The boys tend to need it more than the girls. When clay isn't appropriate because of the lesson, Rita gives the squirmy kids paper and pencils so that they can do something while listening. She finds that many children can listen better if they can make doodles.

➡ *Using Movement to Introduce Lessons:* In order to explain the concepts of realism and abstraction to third graders, Rita introduced them to the idea of a continuum. She had them place themselves physically on a tall-to-short continuum. The physical movement stimulated them as they placed themselves and made corrections. The following lesson went smoothly because the students understood the concept, and the movement involved gave them a break from listening.

➡ *Breaks:* At all ages, stretch breaks and sixty-second movement breaks are very helpful. Chris Christopher sometimes has students in his high school math classes walk out one door of the classroom and back in the other to break up the day. He also gives periodic thirty-second or one-minute stretch breaks. He finds that the students' minds refocus on the subject better.

8. SENSITIVITY AND GROUP DYNAMICS Cooperative learning, which is good for all children, is often easier for girls to master. Girls learn while attending to a code of social interaction better than boys do. Boys tend to focus on performing the task well, without as much sensitivity to the emotions of those around them.

Pecking orders (social strata) are very important to boys; they are often fragile learners when they are low in the pecking order. Pecking order is established by physical size, verbal skills, personality, abilities, and other factors. Over the years of schooling, children flow in and out of many pecking orders and generally find themselves at the top in one part of childhood and at the bottom in another. Some children gravitate toward the top of large-scale pecking orders, such as "the most popular." Others gravitate toward the top of small-group pecking orders, such as the chess club.

New research indicates that girls who are not popular, not called on as much, or not seen or heard in general school life may be less likely to fail in school than boys who are not seen or not socially aggressive. Girls who are low in their pecking order often get better grades than boys who are low in their pecking order. Males on the high end of a pecking order secrete less cortisol; males at the bottom end secrete more. Cortisol can sabotage the learning process; it forces the brain to attend to emotional and survival stress rather than intellectual learning.

9. USE OF SYMBOLISM Both girls and boys like pictures, but boys often rely on them in their learning—mainly because they stimulate the right hemisphere, which is where many boys are more developed. Especially in upper grades, boys tend toward symbolic texts, diagrams, and graphs. They like the coded quality better than girls do. Girls tend to prefer written texts. In literature classes, teachers often find boys inclined to make a great deal out of the author's symbolism and imagery patterns, whereas girls ponder the emotional workings of characters.

10. **USE OF LEARNING TEAMS** Both girls and boys benefit from learning teams and group work, with boys tending to create structured teams and girls forming looser organizations. Boys spend less time than girls in managing team process; they pick leaders quickly and focus on goal orientation.

An example of using teams follows:

➡ *Lobbying for Art Selection:* Rita's students were asked to select pieces of art based on different theories of "What Is Art?" Seven hand-held symbols helped them, for example, a light bulb for "art can make you think," a teardrop for "art can make you feel." Teams were formed. Each was asked to agree on a piece of art (which represented the team's consensual theory) for its "new museum." The students presented their arguments to their teams, to try to persuade their teams to agree with their selections. The students enjoyed the opportunity to persuade others and learned about contributing and listening in a small group.

Learning Differences and the Intelligences

Howard Gardner has done research in the kinds of intelligence with which children learn.

Five types of intelligence best demonstrate male-female differences. A gender's dominance in an intelligence style often results, in part, from the other gender's brain hiding its ability in that style. The concealment is not conscious; the brain puts forth what it feels best at, leaving undeveloped (unless significantly aided) what it does not feel as good at. A brain formed toward one kind of intelligence probably never will be as good at another kind, but it can get better at all intelligences with proper stimulation. These differences indicate the need for changes in classrooms to accommodate different types of learners.

1. **TIME AND SEQUENCE INTELLIGENCES** There are three forms of intelligence in this category: remembering the *past,* connecting to the *present,* and anticipating what might come in the *future.* Each requires the ability to rapidly process and communicate sequential information in a timely, orderly manner.

2. LINGUISTIC INTELLIGENCE Linguistic ability usually lies mostly in the left hemisphere of the brain. Language ability is not the same as talking competence; although the two are related, silent self-talk is as important to the learning student as language used for communication with others.

3. MUSICAL INTELLIGENCE Music generally is processed in the right hemisphere, and rhythm is processed in the left hemisphere. Because it is a whole-brain activity, music can be a powerful influence in many aspects of classroom learning (for example, memorizing, expressing emotion, concentrating, and boosting self-esteem). Both males and females show increased musical development, especially at a young age, when they are musically stimulated. The theory of the "Mozart effect"—that playing complex classical music to babies increases development of both hemispheres—may be exaggerated, but it is accurate in terms of whole-brain development.

4. LOGICAL-MATHEMATICAL INTELLIGENCE An enormous range of brain energy and functions (including both hemispheres and the frontal lobes) are involved when brains deal with mathematics and logic, and many students find these subjects to be challenging. Boys are dominant in logical-mathematical intelligence, relying on it more than girls do. After two decades of effort to increase girls' development in math, females are nearly catching up in most types of mathematics. Even though more girls than boys now take math and science classes, boys are still two to four points ahead of girls in math and science scores (according to the U.S. Department of Education), because the higher levels of calculus, chemistry, and physics involve spatials and abstract cognitives.

5. SPACE-AND-PLACE INTELLIGENCES There are two forms of space-and-place intelligences (the nature of space, our place in it, and how we navigate through it). *Spatial* intelligence consists of the tactile and visual abilities to perceive shapes and forms in one's environment. Engineers and architects use spatial intelligence. Normally, spatial intelligence is found in the right hemisphere of the brain.

Bodily-kinesthetic intelligence is the integration needed to perform a large motor task, such as playing soccer. In this integration of brain functions, the basal ganglia (at the base of each hemisphere of the brain) coordinate the sensory and motor systems. Simultaneously, the amygdala (in the lower limbic system) produces emotional triggers for movements. The motor cortex (connected above the inner ear in each hemisphere) helps coordinate the movements of each side of the body. The cerebellum (at the lower back of the brain) coordinates and fine-tunes automatic movement that allows the successful occurrence of an entire action.

Boys have an advantage in that they are active in their learning, are oriented to body movement, and self-stimulate their spatial abilities, thus increasing right-hemisphere development. A disadvantage is that some boys are in everyone's space when they learn, especially in the early grades, when they haven't learned to control their impulses. So they get in trouble for just being boys. It may be necessary to try to calm down spatial boys, but just as often, helping girls toward physical movement in class stimulates their cortical development in spatial intelligence, in the same way that calming boys down so that everyone can read quietly stimulates their left-hemisphere and linguistic development.

Teachers can help boys to learn by understanding normal male energy, allowing physical movement (from appropriate hugs and touch to getting dirty at recess), and directing normal male energy toward academic focus and good character.

Applying Brain-Based Gender Research

Understanding of innate gender differences leads to understanding of important changes needed in our schools. The following presents only a tiny portion of available research but includes all major categories.

Academic Performance and Classroom Behavior

On average, girls study harder for all courses than boys do, and girls choose to take the harder courses in middle school and high school at a higher rate than boys do. Girls receive approximately 60 percent of the As, and boys receive approximately 70 percent of the Ds and Fs. Among students performing in the top fifth of high school grade ranges, 63 percent are girls.

Boys tend to be louder, more physically aggressive, more competitive, and more prone to attention-getting classroom behaviors than are girls. Boys goof off more, are louder, and naturally tend toward impulsive behavior, resulting in more teacher attention going to boys. Males tend to be less mature; females more considered. Girls are quieter in class, more passive than boys, and tend toward sedentary behavior. Females and males are even more different during puberty and adolescence, with many males seeking outward dominance and many females seeking inward excellence. Females also have longer attention spans than males and do not need, as often, to move interactive classroom activity from one subject to the next through verbal dominance and attention strategies.

Although the effort to calm boys down and give girls attention in the classroom is essential, the ultimate standard for a classroom ought not be parity in loudness, raised hands, or dominance. It is better to treat each student with a clear sense of who he or she is and help the student find a personal mode of expression that fits his or her brain system. This is not what we are doing when we over-diagnose ADHD (attention deficit and hyperactivity disorder) and ADD (attention deficit disorder) and drug (mainly male) students with Ritalin.

Reading and Writing Competence

Girls are approximately one and a half years ahead of boys in reading and writing competence, at all school levels, according to the U.S. Department of Education. Boys are dominant in certain aspects of math and science, largely because of their brain structures. Because boys are so far behind in reading and writing, the focus ought to expand from just advocacy of math and science skills for girls to improvement in reading and writing for boys.

Test Scores

Boys score slightly higher than girls on SAT and other college entrance exams. The male brain is better at storing single-sentence information (even trivia) than is the female brain. The male brain holds a visual advantage in working with lists (as in multiple choice) and in making quick, deductive decisions on lists. The female brain thinks more inductively and often needs substantial information to make a decision. This puts the female at a disadvantage in testing that requires very quick decision making in a short time.

Including essay questions (where females hold the advantage), rather than using all multiple-choice questions (where the deductive male brain has the edge) on standardized tests—as the College Board has announced it will do on the SAT I—will help to reduce this gap.

Psychological, Learning, and Behavioral Disorders

Males and females typically experience different disorders, primarily for hormonal and neurological reasons.

More girls than boys experience overt depression and eating disorders in the teen years. The etiology of eating disorders is related to hormonal and brain chemistry, although stimulation of the disorder is often cultural. Females experience a menstrual cycle, with dominance by estrogen or progesterone, which males do not. For every one boy who *attempts* suicide, four girls do.

However, females are less likely to experience a learning, psychiatric, or behavioral disorder. The female brain, emphasizing left-hemisphere development, does not suffer as many attention problems. The female brain uses more cortical areas for more learning functions. If one area of the female brain experiences a slight defect, another makes up for it. Females also secrete more serotonin than males, so are less inclined to hyperactive disorder.

The male brain tends to lateralize its activity—compartmentalizing it in smaller areas of the brain—and, therefore, suffers more learning disorders. Two-thirds of the learning disabled and 90 percent of the behaviorally disabled are boys. They are nearly 100 percent of the most seriously disabled. Girls constitute only 20 percent of ADHD and ADD diagnoses and 30 percent of serious drug and alcohol problems, leaving 80 percent of brain disorders and 70 percent of substance-abuse problems (which indicate covert depression) to boys. For every girl who *actually commits* suicide, four boys do.

Because the male brain lateralizes, a defect in one area of the brain may affect the only area in which a particular learning function is taking place. Special education and alternative education are dominated by boys for this reason. Many boys are misdiagnosed as having ADHD, ADD, and learning disorders because we have not understood their brains or created classrooms that help them deal well with their natural impulsiveness, lateralization of brain activity, left-hemisphere disadvantage, and learning styles.

Both overt depression in girls and covert depression in boys occur, in large part, because we are not creating bonding and attachment communities in our classrooms and schools to the extent that growing children need.

Maturity, Discipline, and Behavior

The maturity gap between boys and girls, especially in the teens, is one of the most pronounced brain-based gaps and may be the most profoundly disabling feature of classroom life. It is the root of many behaviors labeled "defective."

Female hormones mature earlier and guide the girl toward long-term emotional attachments at a time when immature male hormones may guide the boy toward short-term experimental attachments. When teenage intercourse results in pregnancy, it is usually the girl who drops out of school. Many teen mothers seek to care for children as part of their unmentored biological imperative. Ninety percent of fathers in their teens and early twenties abandon the girl and child. Lacking guidance and familial attachment, they seek new attachments.

The maturity gap between boys and girls affects girls in other ways, including harassment of pubescent girls by boys. Cultural and peer pressures to have sex too early affect both males and females.

More impulsive and less mature than the female brain, the male brain gets a boy into far more trouble in class and in school. Boys cause 90 percent of the discipline problems in school, constitute 80 percent of the dropouts, garner the majority of school punishment for immature behavior, and leave school at a higher rate than girls do.

The kind of classroom discipline that works for girls—often inconsistent, at times very friendly, and lacking profound authority—does not work so well for many boys in middle school and early high school. Male hormones are flooding, and many boys mature through elder dominance systems in which intense bonding and authority best manage them until they learn to manage themselves.

Educational Aspirations

Both male and female teenagers in the United States have profound fear of failure—to meet their parents' demands and to compete in school and in the workplace. Boys fear failure more than girls do. The Department of Education has found that, on average, eighth-grade and twelfth-grade girls have higher educational aspirations than boys. A nongovernmental study corroborated this: three-fourths of girls and only two-thirds of boys "believe they will have many opportunities available to them after they graduate" from high school. In fact, 60 percent of college students are female, and college graduation is the most consistent indicator of stable future income.

Athletics and Extracurricular Activities

The majority of sports funding and community support still goes to male athletics. Boys participate more in sports activities; only 37 percent of high school athletes are girls. Conversely, girls are the majority of student-government officials, after-school club leaders, and school-community liaisons. Our studies show that this is mainly a result of the nature of male and female brains. Boys tend to choose interactive social activities that de-emphasize verbalization and emphasize spatials and physical aggression. Girls tend to choose interactive social activities that emphasize verbalization.

Whereas advocacy for girls in sports and boys in other social interactions is essential, 100 percent female participation in athletics isn't neurologically or hormonally realistic. Many girls (and boys) don't like team sports and do not need to be pressured into them. Boys need a great deal of help in directing themselves toward social interactions other than sports, but boys will probably never gravitate as fully as girls do to clubs that promote coeducational verbal interaction.

Cultural Gender Bias

Boys are at the most gender-based disadvantage in our schools. In kindergarten through sixth grade, almost 90 percent of teachers are women, and female learning and teaching styles dominate. Teachers have not received training in male brain development and performance. Most systems rely on less kinesthetic and less disciplined educational strategies than many boys need.

Earlier writers believed that girls were the primary targets of bias in our schools. The lack of a biological foundation to their studies may have been coupled with a desire to deal with anti-female bias in the workplace by "proving" similar bias in the schools. Although boys are called on more than girls in class, much of the attention boys get in class is punitive, not rewarding, and girls who are not called on often outperform the boys.

When asked how they feel about their school experiences, girls are more likely to express negative feelings and to detail negative experiences; boys are more reluctant to share feelings about any experience and to share details about an experience in which they have suffered pain or privation. They like to appear tough. In studies, girls were only slightly more likely than boys to express feelings of privation and bias.

Of course, there are some gender disadvantages to girls. In some classrooms, boys dominate discussions, and the voices of girls are lost. Role modeling in literature is more often male than female, and male heroes dominate. In some schools, good-old-boy networks teach males that they are inherently privileged and bestow advantages on them, especially in access to employment networks.

Sexual Abuse and Violence

Because males primarily victimize other males, boys are about three times more likely than girls to be victims of violence on school property. The area of greater violence against females is sexual harassment. Girls are more often victims of sexual abuse suffered at the hands of teachers, parents, coaches, school staff, and other students.

Although female violence is increasing, males dominate the violence statistics. Boys are brain- and testosterone-driven toward spatial expression of stress; they tend to lash out physically and with more sexual aggression and physical rage than girls. This trend continues through adulthood.

The U.S. Department of Justice found that, as early as first grade, it can be predicted who the offender males will be. Most of these boys are doing poorly in school, which contributes to their self-concepts of shame and inadequacy and their compensatory aggression against others.

The hormonal and neurological factors in male violence and sexual abuse may never change, but our culture must. Teachers must do what they can to better protect both girls and boys. Males need a different school culture—one with closer bonding, smaller classes, more verbalization, less male isolation, better discipline systems, more authority, and more attention to male learning styles. Anti-bullying curricula help students to understand their own internal systems for expressing angry energy, sad energy, and hurt energy.

Bonding and Attachment

A CHILD'S BRAIN NEEDS BONDING AND ATTACHMENT TO FULLY GROW AND LEARN; without attachment, it does not grow well—behaviorally, psychologically, or intellectually.

Preschool and Kindergarten

Brain research shows that a young child learns best from someone (a family member or teacher) with whom the child is intimately attached; the child learns more, not only from that individual but in total learning competence, which remains long after the early years of attachment.

In ancestral communities, children were raised in nurturing groups, generally with a mother and other parenting females and a father and other related males. Women were the main care providers. At least one male usually remained if other males had to travel away from the family. Fathers tended to protect girls and to train boys in "male" behaviors and skills.

Today, children are often attached to groups of strangers in day care, preschool, and kindergarten. Some have nannies; many have only one parent or live with relatives or in foster care. There may be no father or adult male in the family. The lack of intimate attachments has results in every part of child development. The most problematic children generally come from families in which attachment is lax, dysfunctional, or dangerous. Such children are under great emotional stress and have a hard time learning. To help their brains to learn, we must first deal with the stresses.

Handling Children's Emotional Stress

In this age group, stress generally stems from fear of attachment loss. In the neurological path of attachment loss, the stress hormone (cortisol) rises, flooding the brain and making some neural activity slower (for example, in learning centers in the top of the brain) and other activity quicker (in the brain stem and lower limbic system, where anger and fight-or-flight responses increase). Areas in the hippocampus, where much memory occurs, "fill up" with memory associated with emotional stress, signaling the limbic system to increase stress responses. Other lessons are not retained, and the limbic system keeps the whole brain distracted.

There are some differences in how boys' and girls' brains and hormones handle attachment stress in the early years. Crying is very common, but many boys have already begun to mask pain with "I'm fine." Many girls have begun to mask pain by increasing responsibility behavior, for example, becoming more responsible for younger children or being teacher's helpers. Kindergarten girls complain that they are too fat and suffer body-image distortion. Attachment-stressed boys engage in physical aggression and have greater language delay. Teachers note quick-to-anger and quick-to-withdraw responses from boys and girls.

In early childhood, boys have general learning difficulties, while girls have specific difficulties (for example, in arithmetic). The preschool environment tends to give girls learning advantages and boys disadvantages. There is some research evidence that the male brain is more fragile than the female; it does not return to stability and learning readiness as quickly as the female brain does after a traumatic experience or emotional stress, such as a problem at home in the morning. This may be more true the younger the brain is; more boys than girls have learning, emotional, and behavioral difficulties in preschool and kindergarten.

Bonding and Attachment Solutions

CLASS SIZE AND NUMBER OF TEACHERS Brain-based research indicates that, for learning purposes, the presence of two teachers is optimal. We recommend one teacher for every eight or ten students. With two teachers, the class can be fifteen or twenty students. If there are any serious behavioral problems among the students, an additional person—a "roaming" teacher who is trained in special education—can work with the stressed child.

This student-teacher ratio has a positive effect on academic learning, psychosocial learning, discipline, and general growth. It allows teachers to attend to the gender-different learning needs of boys and girls. For example, one teacher can monitor children engaged in a physical task, such as construction or art, while another can be involved with children in a writing or reading activity.

BONDING RITUALS Bonding rituals are important in preschool and kindergarten to help to offset the impact of lack of attachment, especially with boys who have intellectual, language, and social delays. The following are some examples:

➡ *High Five:* Kathi Winkler notes that bonding with boys can be more difficult when most of the school staff are females who are not comfortable with "male" activities, such as wrestling and roughhousing. Her most popular innovation with boys is the "high five." Thrusting out her palm, she says, "Gimme five." The child does so; then Kathi puts her palm up high and says, "Up high." The child high-fives, and Kathi lowers her hand and says, "Down low." As the child moves his hand to meet hers, she quickly pulls back and says, "Whoops, too slow!" as the child misses her hand.

Two elements of this help in bonding with harder-to-reach kids—usually males. Boys seem to like the physical connection of a high five better than a hug. Second, the game has an element of competition that makes it a challenge; boys participate in it over and over in an attempt to not be too slow. They become excited as they begin to succeed. Using the game in nonconfrontational moments allows Kathi to begin to establish a positive relationship that transfers to more difficult moments.

➡ *Name Songs:* To help build attachment, Kathi uses each child's name as she dismisses the class at the end of the day. She sings the "banana" song from "The Name Game" ("Toby, Toby bo boby. Fe fi mo moby—Toby") or "The Little Box" ("If I had a little red box, to put my Alan in, I'd take him out and [kiss, kiss, kiss] and put him back in again"). Kathi lets each child select the "banana" or "box" song; if "box" is chosen, the child may name the color of the box.

➡ *Feeling Board:* Have a permanent "feeling cork board" on which balloons are taped above the words "angry," "sad," "happy," and "mad." Let the kids throw safe, plastic darts at the feelings they are having, which gives them an action for accessing and then talking about the feelings.

➡ *Personalizing:* Personalize the child's desk, coat hook, and other storage areas to increase the sense of attachment and identity with the environment.

➡ *Celebrate Successes:* Have portable and digital (immediate-result) cameras around and take pictures of the children being successful at a task; they can admire the pictures later. This especially seems to help young girls feel good about what they're doing.

➡ *Use Group Work:* Help facilitate working groups and teams in which girls learn to take a leadership role; this also obliges them to work out their in-crowd, out-crowd arguments with one another.

➡ *Give Praise:* Praise more than you think you need to, especially girls, for accomplishing activities well.

➡ *Include Quiet Girls:* Make sure not to miss the hidden high energy of girls, who may pull back because a few loud boys dominate; help these girls become leaders.

MENTORING It is important for children to have ongoing, caring relationships with positive adult role models who are not their parents and to see how responsible adults interact. This is especially important for children from single-parent, non-parent, and dysfunctional households.

Mentors help to boost children's self-esteem. A thirty-two-year study of children in Kauai, Hawaii, showed that children from homes in which there was poverty, alcoholism, divorce, and other serious problems had a much better chance of making a good transition to adulthood if there was a caring adult available to them outside the family.

Mentors listen to children and serve as neutral ears (especially with kids who feel that they can't confide in their parents). Mentors can add new points of view, new explorations of talents and interests, and new career possibilities. They can discuss and reinforce values and help kids to form responsible, thoughtful conclusions on their own.

➡ *Role-Model Mentors:* Bring in male mentors from the community, or boys from upper grades, to promote male presence—especially to make male role models available to fatherless boys. Bring in female role models to help girls develop healthy self-images.

ROUTINES AND SCHEDULES Bonding rituals work especially well when framed by other daily routines, such as taking off outdoor shoes and putting on indoor shoes. All preschool and kindergarten classrooms benefit from rituals and schedules. The young brain needs freedom to discover but also needs an ordered environment in which to learn. Classrooms that include one or more children with a learning or behavioral difficulty benefit especially from routines and schedules.

➡ *Create Consistency:* A kindergarten boy had serious behavioral problems. After his parents' divorce, the time the boy spent with his father was no longer consistent. Special education teacher Carrie Whalley and other teachers worked at keeping the boy on a schedule during the day in order to offset his lack of stability at home.

➡ *Bonding Tips:* Principal Debbie Hughes and her staff devised this list of tips, which apply to children of all age groups:

- Be genuine with children
- Call each child by name
- Learn about the child's world, personal life, and personal interests
- Use "I noticed . . ." statements
- Smile, touch (when appropriate), and make eye contact
- Attend events in the child's life whenever possible
- Respect the child and the child's opinions
- Personally disclose stories of your life, as appropriate

- Be nonjudgmental
- Listen and then listen some more
- Give the child choices and options that compel healthy decision making
- Admit mistakes you have made

Elementary School

Children's brains cannot learn and work fully unless the children feel the stability and comfort of profound one-on-one bonds with teachers and other mentors. Many kids have trouble learning because they don't feel cared about. Bonding helps to reduce discipline problems and increase educational success.

As elementary school classrooms grow larger, there are decreased opportunities for teacher-student bonding. Bonding and attachment activities in elementary schools, especially for fourth grade and above, also suffer because of the idea that the more time taken away from instruction, the less well students perform on year-end testing and in middle school and beyond. In fact, often the way to better academic performance is not instruction but love and attention.

Bonding is the least measurable way to ensure good learning. It takes time and effort. It needs the support of the whole educational system. As more research emerges in the field of emotional literacy, and as more children suffer from lack of adequate bonding, schools will be forced to create bonding throughout each classroom day.

Some research says that girls' self-esteem is lowered because girls are called on less than boys are. Our research shows that, although boys are likely to receive more attention from the teacher, it is negative attention because they are noisier and more disruptive. Attention to girls may be less moment-by-moment, but it is generally more positive. Being called on in class is only one indicator of bonding among teachers and students.

Bonding and Attachment Activities

The following are innovations teachers use to increase bonds and improve learning for elementary school boys and girls:

➡ *Personal Greetings:* Each morning, Carol Myers gives her fourth-grade students some directions or a problem to think about as she greets them individually, with eye contact and a handshake or a hug.

➡ *"Good Things" List:* At the beginning of the year, the class talks about how to work as a successful family, especially in respecting others. For the next couple of weeks and periodically throughout the year, the students and Carol write on a paper chart at the front of the room "good things" they see people doing or saying to one another. Students get to see their names in print in a positive way and they practice written language.

➡ *"Yays and Yucks":* Each student has an opportunity every day to say positive and negative things that have happened the day before or may happen. A student may choose to pass, and a time limit can be established. This helps to build relationships within the classroom and provides Carol with insight about each student's home life.

➡ *Physical Activity:* At the beginning of the school year, Carol participates in some physical activity with her class (for example, running, climbing a rope, playing kickball). She makes sure it is something she can do well and compete with the boys. This helps her to earn a new and different kind of respect from the students, particularly the boys.

➡ *Cheers:* Stacy Moyer does a cheer using the children's names, for example, "Two, four, six, eight, who do we appreciate? Jose, Jose, hooray!"

➡ *Working with Parents:* Jenny Peterson sees improvement in learning and discipline when troublesome students realize that Jenny cares about them and is working with their parents to help them improve. She tries to help the students to tell her what they need from her. Some students have lost trust in a teacher/adult, and it takes a while to rebuild that.

➡ *Encouraging Parent-Child Learning:* Monica Miller encourages her students' parents to do learning activities with their children at home, such as cutting up old magazines with scissors; coloring with crayons; taking nature walks and discussing what has been seen; sorting beans, noodles, and buttons;

asking the child to name four red things, four blue things, and so on, in the grocery store; and dressing dolls to learn how to button, zip, tie, and lace.

➡ *Tutoring/Homework Club:* Lois J. Hedge and a coworker conduct a tutoring/homework help club once a week after school for fifth- and sixth-graders, mostly boys who are easily distracted and/or have some behavioral problems and are not completing their work during class time. The students are signed into the class by their parents. The teachers give lots of positive feedback. The boys especially seem to like the small group. They open up more to the teachers and one another. Their attitudes toward getting their work done improve.

➡ *Journal Writing:* Julie Ogilvie uses journal writing for bonding in third and fourth grade. One activity is based on a song that says, "Friends forever, till the end / On this my friend, you can depend / When you are weak, I'll be strong / When I fall back, won't you pull me along." The students write what they think that means.

➡ *Team-Building Activities:* Julie also uses team-building activities to build trust. The students and she talk about what the students expect of their classmates and teacher and what she expects of them.

➡ *Mothers and Daughters Group:* Susan Colgan, a family-involvement co-ordinator, describes a successful after-school program for fourth-grade girls and their mothers, who participate in craft and cooking classes, field trips, and other activities. The final event is a dinner at a restaurant. Two teachers serve as role models to the mothers and daughters.

Handling Students' Emotional Stress

The decrease in family bonding creates emotional stress in students. A stressed student acts out, causing disturbance or withdrawing, in an unconscious effort to make sure the other students and the teacher experience the stress with him. Brain-based research indicates that a great deal of intellectual intelligence depends on emotional intelligence. Teachers must deal with the emotional stresses in the child's life before the mind can be educated.

Girls and boys often differ in how they "announce" their stress. Girls tend toward increased passivity (acting in) and boys toward increased aggressiveness (acting out). However, many boys passively watch their grades decline, their friendships wither, and their levels of depression increase; and many girls curse, hit, and rebel against authority. When asked to draw what they thought about when under stress, most boys drew about war, space ships, or violent things; the girls tended to draw food or their play area. Even in first grade, girls can be heard to say that they are fat. This is rare among boys.

➡ *Ask Girls Open-Ended Questions:* Maxine Meyer, a third-grade teacher, says, "Anger in girls often masks a severe rejection of the self and an enormous sense of loss." Maxine uses a lot of open-ended questions, and she listens to the answers, without guiding discussion too heavily, in order to encourage girls to find out what's behind their anger. Girls generally talk enough, she finds, to lead themselves to answers.

➡ *Ask Boys Guiding Questions:* With boys, teachers often find it fruitful to ask questions that help the boys to answer (for example, "Has someone hurt you today?"; "Were you just in a fight with [so-and-so]?"). These questions are directed and concrete, and discussion is often led by the teacher, not the child. With boys, this often works as a mitigator to the inherent slowness in the male brain's processing of emotive information. The teacher helps by trying to point the child in a specific direction in order to find the emotional material hidden there.

Rita Rome saw a change in behavior in a fourth grader whom she had taught since kindergarten. Suspecting that his acting out indicated unhappiness, she asked him, "If you could make a wish to change something in your life, what would you wish for?" The answer to such a question is usually revealing.

DEALING WITH PROJECTION STRESS One key area of student stress that heavily affects learning is student-teacher stress, resulting from transference onto the teacher of environmental stressors, such as child-parent stress, an absent parent, poverty, and lack of extended-family support.

Boys and girls deal with major stress in different ways. Boys usually act out through power struggles. Jenny Peterson taught a boy whose father had committed suicide; because the boy was now the man of the house, he was trying to be the man of the classroom, in control.

While boys aim to get attention, girls tend to sit down and get to work, to please the teacher. Many girls also talk out stresses among their friends or with the person who is the source of the stress.

It takes maturity and restraint for teachers to interact effectively with stressed children. It helps to identify family stresses that affect the child, and it often requires help from parents and counseling professionals. Teachers cannot solve all student stresses. A teacher can try to guide a child (and, often, the child's family) toward solutions; but the teacher's ultimate job is to help the child learn to manage his or her own stress wisely. In this way, the teacher mentors the higher character of the child (self-esteem), removes blockages to academic learning by removing distracting stress, and teaches valuable life-survival skills. Here are some innovations that teachers are using:

➡ *Stress Balls:* Denise Young's class makes stress balls out of round, fairly large balloons filled with soft items, such as flour, rice, and beans. These are kept in a basket by her desk. When a child is stressed or nervous, he or she can ask for a stress ball.

➡ *Run an Errand:* When a student is ready to "blow," the teacher asks him to run to another room (across the building) to get a book. The teacher there knows to tell him that she loaned it to someone else. She sends the child there, and so on. The child is sent to four or five places, and the book is never found. All this running around seems to get rid of the aggression the child is feeling. By the time he returns to the classroom, the child usually has calmed down.

➡ *Allowing Movement in the Classroom:* Teachers often find it helpful to let a child move around the room while he is trying to think of something or talk about emotional content. The male brain does not move neurotransmission in the upper limbic areas as fast as the female brain; nor does it as naturally direct emotional material between the right and left brain hemispheres for analysis and verbalization. Physical movement in class—with rules about what movement is and is not acceptable—is a powerful asset in managing stress and it stimulates imagination and learning because of increased blood flow in the neocortex of the child's brain. Movement of glucose also increases in limbic areas of the brain, where emotional processing occurs. Engaging the whole body in the task of emotional processing seems to enhance neurotransmission to limbic (emotive) and left-brain (verbal) areas.

Boys need to move more than girls—even just standing up or walking around a table. When a boy punches a bag, does karate kicks, or rides his bicycle fast when he is angry, sad, or frustrated, the boy is naturally moving energy through his brain by moving his whole body.

Use of movement is also important with girls, especially when a girl is blocked in her emotional processing or cannot release her stress through traditional sitting-and-talking strategies.

Jenny Peterson allows some movement when kids are working, but not when she's teaching. She can now tell "thinking" movement from "trouble" or "stress" movement.

➡ *Talking About Feelings:* Teachers can engage kids in talking about feelings. Boys can cry and talk about their feelings; they just don't do it as easily as girls do. Some teachers have instituted a talk-based check-in time at the beginning of their classes, for about five minutes, in which all students have to say something about how they are feeling. This can reduce emotional stress and open the rest of the class time to learning. A student may say, "I'm all right, I guess," but the teacher can tell otherwise, and after lesson activities have begun, the teacher takes that student aside for another five minutes or so of talk.

The Role of the Mentor

When we think of improvement in bonding, attachment, and trust in the classroom, we often think of what the teacher can do. Yet other allies are available, including the student body and the families of students.

➡ *Intergenerational (Vertical) Mentoring Between Grade Levels:* Kimberly Walter describes a program in which each first grader has a fifth-grade "study buddy." The two children eat lunch together many days of the week. The fifth-graders are trained by the teachers to be responsible for things such as instructing the first-graders in proper etiquette. Kimberly reports that although the fifth-graders sometimes feel frustrated by the responsibility, they are more than thrilled to live up to the role-model expectation.

Carrie Whalley has found that even fifth- and sixth-grade students from bad environments are positively influenced by the opportunity to help primary-grade students. The older child's natural propensity for compassion and service shines for the younger student, who becomes like a younger relative. Carrie says that comparing the school environment to a family is very important, especially for children who do not get enough attention at home or who see themselves as failures. They need to reframe themselves as people who can be successful.

Another teacher discovered that even the boys with discipline problems "turn themselves around when working with their kindergarten buddies." Part of the success comes from emphasis on the importance of the student being a good role model, not just in the kindergarten classroom but also in the hallways and lunchroom.

➡ *Teacher-Team Collaboration:* In Carrie's school, a team of teachers meets once a month to assist teachers who need strategies for dealing with problem students. They come up with many ways that teachers and students can form relationships with those children. One example was to have a fifth-grade boy who was experiencing academic and behavioral problems go into a kindergarten classroom to help out during reading instruction. His reading skills were enhanced by helping younger students, and it helped him to feel good about himself.

Carrie notes that the elementary years are a critical time when a boy will choose a "clan" to grow up in. "Teachers can be part of a boy's clan, steering him in the right direction. Female teachers can help link up boys to positive male role models in the school and in the community."

MENTORS FROM THE COMMUNITY Finding mentors is not difficult, especially if the community is trained to realize the importance of parents, grandparents, coaches, scout leaders, clergy, aunts and uncles, and other responsible and caring adults in a child's life. Many schools require volunteer time from adult family members of students. The bonds that participants establish with the school and teachers, as well as with the students, more than compensate for the time.

➡ *The Reading Tutorial:* The simplest use of adult volunteer mentors is the reading tutorial. Parents, grandparents, and others come to class for an hour or two a week to read to and with elementary students.

➡ *Visits from Professionals:* Professionals can come into the classroom to share stories of their lives and work. Police officers and lawyers can help kids understand facts about personal safety, automobile safety, laws, truancy, tagging, vandalism, juvenile justice, effects of gang involvement, drugs, and so on. Theater people can help to stage and direct student productions. Some professional groups "adopt a class."

THE NEED FOR MALE ROLE MODELS The presence of fathers and grandfathers in classrooms is extremely valuable for both boys and girls—especially for boys brought up without fathers. Jenny Peterson notes that boys who have good male role models don't get into as much trouble. They seem to have a certain level of security and code of behavior that the students without fathers don't have. The latter boys seem to display more aggressive behavior, as if they need to be in charge and put others down so they can feel powerful. "There's no one to show them what it means to be a man or what having power means; they're trying to figure it out on their own."

Father hunger is also a problem in the area of character development for girls. Girls who are raised without a father's love and discipline can overwhelm teachers with what Jan Miller calls "lack of a moral compass."

To provide children with the father images they need, schools may have to increase male-mentoring opportunities. Schools and teachers must ask fathers and grandfathers to come in to fill this gap.

➡ *Fathers Sharing Insights and Experiences:* Be sure that there are men in the boys' educational life, especially from fifth grade onward. Tracy Sharp, a remedial reading teacher, stresses the need for boys to connect with male role models and books that have male characters. One year, she asked a father to portray the lion from *The Wizard of Oz.* She was teaching the difference between a question and a statement, so the students had to interview the lion. Another year, a father shared his experience of living with an African tribe.

Middle School

The Early Adolescent's Drop in Self-Esteem

Children in middle school are hungry for the stability of bonds. Middle school and high school children feel their attachments deeply, and attachment loss can be disabling for them. Most middle school children feel that they must have attachments to survive, and this feeling confuses them as they strive to be independent of adults. They also tend to be super-sensitive and take things hard.

A child's emotional well-being is a foundation of learning, and middle school children typically experience a drop in self-esteem. Brain-based research helps to explain why this happens.

- The brain and the body are growing at such a rapid pace that natural psychological equilibria are thrown off course for a period of at least two to four years.
- Leaps in cognition and abstraction, especially in the top of the brain, show the child that he or she is very small and the world is very large; thus, the child's innocence falls away, leaving behind a fear of not belonging, not being good enough, and not having the capacity to make it in the world.
- A cognitive leap invades emotional development by creating a state of overreaction in which even a small emotional hiccup can become a major thing.
- Individuation—the process of becoming independent of parents—is a whole-brain experience that requires a large complex of neural networks. This upsets earlier equilibria at the time when the upper brain must master difficult math, language, and other abstract skills as well as learn new technologies. Furthermore, other attachment safety nets—such as the extended family, religious communities, and rites of passage—often are absent, leaving the child vulnerable to becoming overstimulated by the internal independence process but unprotected by external guidance systems.
- The brain often seeks independence in ways that alienate parents. They often say of a middle schooler, "He wants to be on his own" or "She doesn't need me as much anymore," reading only the off-putting signal the child is sending (perhaps reading it conveniently). This leaves the child, who is far needier of bonds than it appears, alienated from the primary caregivers.

Teachers play a crucial role in this, and they play it more strongly than a generation ago. The extended family and other support systems are now rare. For many middle schoolers, the teacher is one of the most stable presences in their lives. Even for those who have stable family systems, the teacher is a significant mentor. A mentor's attachment can be salvation to the mind and soul of a child in need. Some show their need for attachment to a teacher by anger; others demonstrate sadness, silence, or attention-getting devices.

Teachers know that it is easier to teach students who are bonded to them. Many have created innovations that help them bond with middle school students and help the students keep their self-esteem. Self-esteem can be bolstered a little through external practices (for example, making sure to call on everyone in the class every day so that no one feels left out), but these practices cannot satisfy the brain, which needs ritual. This is especially true of students with problems. Calling on them in class does not satisfy their needs for bonding and help with emotional stress. Learning is difficult for them because their brains' limbic systems are clouded by emotional stress and the stress hormone, cortisol. As the limbic system strives to manage the emotional stress, it doesn't let the rest of the brain, especially the four lobes on top, learn in the way the classroom demands.

Handling Students' Emotional Stress

Important in the area of bonding are one-on-one attention and other rituals. Another key is educating children about their own mental and emotional processes. Middle school students are capable of high abstraction and deep interpersonal observation. If we focus them on areas of difficulty and educate them on how to help themselves, they will.

PROBLEMS IN PRIMARY ATTACHMENT RELATIONSHIPS Every school has children whose families are suffering upheaval from divorce, death, abandonment, trouble with the law, or abuse. These children are living with attachment trauma, which affects their ability to learn. Teachers profoundly touch students' lives when they understand and mentor their attachment traumas.

PEER HUMILIATION The level of girl-girl, boy-boy, and cross-sex humiliation has risen in the last generation. Young people are very hard on one another, especially in the early to mid-teens. From a biological point of view, adolescent peer humiliation is necessary: human survival depends on young people ferreting out one another's weaknesses. They help one another, sometimes through aggressive provocation, to resolve personal flaws.

Many school districts have instituted zero-tolerance policies regarding peer harassment or humiliation by students. This goal will never be met because evolutionary biology resists it. But just as increasing one-on-one teacher presence is required to help with students under terrible stress at home, so is it required to help educate students on what they are doing to each other and why. Here are some key areas middle schoolers need to be taught more about:

The Child Who Doesn't Fit His or Her Gender Type. Many adolescent boys and girls experience a biological pull toward the mass group, in masculine and feminine directions, because of biology and socialization. This causes profound emotional stress for those who have what we call "bridge" brains—in the center of the male-female brain continuum. There are boys who feel as much girlish as boyish, and girls who feel as much boyish as girlish. There are sensitive boys and aggressive girls. Attention to the needs of these students is critical.

The nuancing of the human brain is perhaps the most complex of any species, and middle school is the time when nuance becomes extremely important to the child. We must guide girls and boys beyond stereotypes, into nuance. Teachers need to talk about gender stereotypes in nearly every area of study, from science to gym class, from math to literature.

➡ *Using Visual Media:* Many teachers find the visual media useful in this regard. They show video clips of movies, television shows, and commercials, leading students to understand how our culture tries to create gender uniformity, and then leading them to see through the uniformity to individuality. This kind of ongoing mentoring relieves a great deal of stress, especially for the bridge-brained boys and girls.

Inadequate Social Skills and Maturity Expectations. It is immensely stressful for a child to have inadequate understanding of what is expected of him or her by peers and elders. Early adolescent students ask (verbally and nonverbally) crucial questions of themselves and their peers. The more we help them toward mature answers, the less distracted their brains are and the more maturely they engage in bonding and learning.

➡ *Peer Dilemmas:* "Peer dilemmas" are scenarios that students can discuss and resolve. Here are some adapted from the teen magazine *REACT:*

- Someone in the in-crowd has just asked you to have lunch, but you already had made plans to meet your best friend. What is the right thing to do in this situation?

- The class bully picks on you repeatedly. What should your friends do?
- A friend begs you to get booze from your parents' liquor cabinet. When you say you won't, your friend becomes angry. What should you do?
- Your friend is having a party and you're not invited. What should you do?
- You tell your friend a secret about yourself and then discover that she has told others. What should you do?
- Your friend has hurt your feelings. How long should you wait for an apology? If you don't get one, should you reach out? If so, when and how?
- Should you always be honest with your friends?
- Is peer pressure always a part of your life? Should you expect to find friends who do not try to pressure you toward bad things?

➡ *Specific Classes:* Some schools help students to handle emotional stress by teaching classes in emotion, ethics, and social skills (for example, using peer dilemmas).

➡ *Counseling and Teaching Approaches:* Counselors (and many teachers) tend to rely on words to a greater extent than many boys are comfortable with. To many boys, asking them to come to a counselor's office or sit down and talk indicates personal weakness.

➡ *Peripatetic Counseling:* The Socratic model of walking and teaching allows the mentor and student to do something physical together. This is good for stimulation of the limbic system and emotional processing in any child, especially boys. It creates opportunities for objects and people along the way to play a role in the counseling process (for example, "What does that guy over there remind you of?"; "What do you think that woman is feeling right now?") and it takes counseling into the larger world.

➡ *Quick Tension-Release Techniques:* Emotion-management innovations especially help middle school boys, who are often hard to manage.

- *Stress Balls:* When a student needs to calm down and talk to her, Darla Novick lets the student use a stress ball to have something to do as he or she talks. Boys especially are able to talk and express their feelings better.

- *Drawing:* Darla allows students to draw while they're talking. Giving them something to do helps them to process better.
- *Quick-Release Techniques:* Aware of the effect of testosterone on boys' behavior, Brandy Barnett realizes that trying to discuss things and problem solve with them usually doesn't work. They would rather blame, yell, and shut down to handle their anger. So she teaches them appropriate ways to quick-release their tension (ripping paper, hitting a pillow, and so forth). This helps them calm down; then she uses stress balls and verbal processing.

➡ *Care Teams:* Brandy's school uses care teams to meet students' needs to feel bonded to others. After-school activities and care teams provide mentors and counseling staff. Each student bonds with at least one teaching-team member.

➡ *Cooperative Learning:* Brandy creates bonds between students by using a series of cooperative learning activities before attempting anything academic.

➡ *Four-Step Method:* This method works well in increasing bonds between teachers and students. Teachers can also help increase bonds between students by letting them pair up and then training them in this process:

1. Ask questions (for example, about how they want to spend class time)
2. Listen carefully to the answers
3. Find common ground
4. Do something together (follow through on the action decision)

Community Collaboration

Teachers alone cannot meet all students' bonding needs. Middle schools often desperately need the help of parents and other adults. Unfortunately, parents often assume that "Middle school kids don't want their parents around." Although students may posture this, their physical, psychosocial, and cognitive brain development needs a wide variety of attachments and bonds. Even if a middle school child doesn't want a parent in the school, all students can benefit from the mentoring of other elders, businesspeople, older youths and adults from faith communities, high school seniors, college students, and other mentors in specific life skills.

Teachers may want to refer parents to Bernard Goldberg's book, *Bias: A CBS Insider Exposes How the Media Distort the News.* In the chapter "The Most Important Story You Never Saw on TV," Goldberg talks about the steady decline in the behavioral, emotional, and physical health of children in the United States that has occurred with the increase of latchkey children and children in day care. Examples are

- From 1979 to 1988, the suicide rate for girls aged ten to fourteen rose 27 percent; for boys it rose 71 percent.
- In 1970, only one in twenty girls in the United States under the age of fifteen had engaged in sexual relations; today one in three is the norm.
- Three million U.S. teenagers contract sexually transmitted diseases each year.
- A study of five million eighth-graders found that children who are left home alone more than eleven hours per week are three times more likely to abuse drugs, alcohol, or tobacco than are kids with after-school adult supervision.

Although some parents have no choice but to go to work, Goldberg is alarmed that the focus of many parents is on making more money for material goods and status, rather than on providing care and direction for their children.

The Hearst Foundation asked students for their reasons for having achieved success; respondents called parental support "the biggest factor" in their success. This reported outcome continued through high school.

➡ *Informal Role Playing:* Sex education is a specific area where help is needed. Many parents don't teach it. Community-group mentors can help to alleviate the burden on the teacher through specific classes in appropriate sexual behavior. Through informal role playing, students can practice appropriate responses. For example, girls can practice "saying no without hurting the other person's feelings."

➡ *Rites of Passage:* Scout organizations, faith communities, and other groups help to provide valuable rite-of-passage experiences for youths. Unfortunately, these are not available to many students. Community-sponsored safety and first-aid courses, presented in the school, are examples of opportunities for youths to experience achievement and "graduation."

➡ *Mentoring and Role Modeling:* Bring in a mentor from the community for every young person who needs one. Make sure that every girl has at least one female role model in the school to bond with and look up to. Have male role models and mentors talk with boys about ideas and stories that demonstrate what it means to "be a man," that is, an adult male who is essential to his community's care and development.

➡ *Downward Mentoring:* Lilly Figueroa paired middle school students with first-grade students. At first, the older students read to the younger ones; as they bonded, it became a deeper relationship. At the end of the year,

each middle school student made a "book" and presented it to the younger student. They felt good about seeing the younger students look up to them.

Match every middle school student who is capable of mentoring with an elementary or preschool student. Consider making mentoring a homework assignment.

High School

The brain is still growing in adolescence; it needs bonding and attachment from caregivers to grow, and the primary intergenerational bonding groups for the growing brain are family (parents, extended family, and non-blood kin) and educators.

By high school, peer bonding groups have a more profound effect on brain development than they did when the child was younger. Nonetheless, the adolescent still relies a great deal on parenting and educational models. Chris Christopher, who teaches high school math, notes that students come to school with many more problems than previous generations did. He says that teachers need to know the backgrounds of their students and be careful about what they say. They need to talk to parents and build trust with students, because the school is sometimes a haven for students who have problems at home: "You need to show every student that he or she is important."

Showing Interest in Students

The adolescent brain wants love from teachers, not just instruction, so how well students learn sometimes is dependent on how they feel about their teachers. High school students have described good teachers as those who "got into their minds" and bad ones as those who didn't. They say that the teachers they liked knew how to talk to them as women and men, not just as kids, and were good role models. Memory is enhanced if an adolescent feels emotionally cared for.

➡ *Showing Students You Care:* Chris Christopher usually stands at his door when his students arrive and greets them all, sometimes asking questions, such as: "How's the day going?" or "Did you see that movie you were talking about?" He listens and picks up little things about the students and then talks to them about their interests and their classroom difficulties. This tells the students that he cares about them and that they are special. He adds that if he didn't really care, this method wouldn't work. He also gives students his e-mail address so they can contact him about questions and concerns.

➡ *Interest Cards:* Chris has each student fill out a card on the first day of class, indicating the student's math experience and personal interests. After a few weeks of interaction with the students, he brings out the cards and knows what to discuss with them. For example, if a student is interested in a particular television show, he asks the student questions about recent episodes. Such conversations are the beginnings of bonds with students.

➡ *Check-In Time:* Allow check-in and talk time in human growth and development, social studies, psychology, and other applicable classes, in which students have a chance to verbalize issues they face, including harassment, depression, and bullying.

Communication and Conflict Resolution

It is never a good idea to communicate in a way that criticizes adolescents' work, behavior, or appearance. The more they are criticized, the more students become the "bad" people teachers describe or expect. Research shows that high school teachers tend to withhold approval and attachment when children do not behave in ways that meet the teachers' gender stereotypes. This has a dysfunctional result for the students' development and the teacher-student relationships.

High school students need to look good in front of their peers. When a teacher criticizes or chastises an adolescent in front of his or her peers, the teacher is asking for trouble. Studies show that when a teacher and student enter a conflict, a boy tends to use a louder voice and fewer words, while a girl favors more words. The intention of the hurt student is to return to a position of respect in front of the peers, and to do so by dominating or defying the teacher, who is perceived as the betrayer of respect and a bond.

➡ *Begin with Something Positive:* Rather than giving her negative feedback with which to chastise herself, one of Patricia Henley's teachers looked for ways to make initial positive remarks, such as "I really liked the way you described the main character in your essay. Perhaps you could use some of the same kind of words to describe the plot of the story, as well."

➡ *Keeping It Private:* If a student's behavior or work needs to be addressed, and the problem is not major, the teacher can speak to the student about it in private, thereby allowing the student to maintain his or her dignity.

➡ *Apologizing:* When ego conflicts emerge between a teacher and student for which the teacher can apologize, sometimes eliciting a student apology in return, an immense teaching moment occurs. This is especially true if the teacher has the trust and respect of the students. If the teacher does not, increased bonding activities are important.

➡ *Bonding Activities:* A "ropes" course can be an effective student-teacher bonding activity, especially with nonverbal boys. In both wilderness and urban settings, trained ropes-course supervisors help build student-and-teacher teams through a combination of exercises on ropes and poles, rock-wall climbing, and group-trust rituals.

Simple activities that build trust and bonding between students can be carried out on the school grounds with adequate supervision (for example, in a "trust walk," one student is blindfolded and led on a walk by another student, then the students switch roles, and the walk is repeated in a different direction or with a different path).

➡ *Help Girls' Self-Images:* Many girls do not act out their need for approval and attention, but it is there. To help girls at this critical stage of life, teachers can carry high expectations and offer even more encouragement than appears necessary.

➡ *Communication and Conflict-Resolution Training:* Make sure each student participates, as needed, in conflict-resolution and communication training.

Peer Leadership, Not Peer Pressure

The peer-leadership program was born of concern in the medical community, which has found in brain-based research an understanding of the neu-

rological and psychosocial need to reduce student stress and increase psychological health. Teenagers' heart rates, EEGs, and other internal stress monitors change in response to stressors. Students feeling pressure and stress need support and assistance in order to "learn through" the stress and maintain behavioral standards. Peer-leadership programs help students support one another to diminish stresses that lead to high-risk behavior, violence, and dropping out of school.

Mentoring

Anthony, a music teacher, spent more time with students he believed needed additional support and mentoring, and he visited their other classes. Many were young men who had no fathers or mentors. A colleague said that one student was disrupting class. Anthony met with the student, who seemed re-calcitrant and wanted to know what business it was of his. Anthony said that he was concerned that this student be successful in all his classes. They talked for some time. Later, the teacher who had been having trouble with the student told Anthony that his discussion with the student resulted in improvement. The student had bonded with Anthony and would listen to him.

Teachers can be trained to be mentors. A mentor bonds with students, is a primary role model, and treats them as an extended family member would, pushing them, listening to them, and—when appropriate—letting them go.

➡ *Existing Programs:* Big Brothers Big Sisters has a school-based mentoring program that can help schools teach the art of mentoring. High school students are matched with elementary students under the tutorship of adults.

A Michigan program called KUDOS, sponsored by Phi Delta Kappa, a professional service organization of African American educators, accepts students from the ninth to twelfth grades who maintain a 2.0 GPA. The KUDOS club meets weekly from September to June. The adult leader facilitates activities that build social and academic skills, recreational opportunities, and character-development discussions, and leads students in working through personal issues, from setting goals to sexual responsibility.

H. Stephen Glenn, founder of Capabilities, Inc., and coauthor of *7 Strategies for Developing Capable Students,* has developed an "assets inventory" that is a good resource in how and what to mentor. It offers specific asset-building activities and theories.

➡ *Help in Planning:* Help the teenager refine future options by giving him a mentor's vision of what his strengths and weaknesses are. All high school students should experience such mentoring.

➡ *Male Mentors:* Bring fathers and other male role models into the school to tell their stories and mentor males into healthy manhood.

➡ *Female Mentors:* Bring mothers, grandmothers, and other female mentors and role models into the school to help girls learn sexual and social ethics and hear stories of the female life span and female successes.

Discipline and Related Issues

BOYS TEND TO PRACTICE MORE AGGRESSION NURTURANCE THAN GIRLS, AND GIRLS more empathy nurturance than boys.

Boys and Aggression Nurturance

One type of nurturance involves aggression activities, such as rough physical touch, competitive games, and aggressive talk and nonverbal gestures. The male brain and chemistry impel males to practice less eye-to-eye contact and more shoulder-to-shoulder contact; less empathy and more challenge. Social pressures also push males toward more aggressive behavior and females toward empathic behavior. This often causes males to be labeled as discipline problems in the school.

Research indicates that we need to understand the value of aggression nurturance. Boys, especially, relate by bumping and pushing one another; they build strength, focus, attentiveness, and hierarchy through these actions. This nurturance style increases into elementary school and when hormones (especially testosterone) hit, it soars in the middle teens and twenties.

As the male becomes an adult, he learns additional ways to nurture, including more word-oriented empathy systems. But most males, even in middle age, rely greatly on aggression nurturance. This may cause them relational problems with females and less aggressive males, but it also promotes greater hierarchical success in the workplace.

Preschool and Kindergarten

Dealing with Aggressive Behavior

One of the primary areas of difficulty in the preschool and kindergarten classroom is aggressive behavior, which has inspired a great deal of medication use. Boys are generally more physically aggressive than girls, and girls are generally more socially manipulative than boys.

Preschool and kindergarten children's brains and bodies are growing rapidly, making them especially sensitive to aggression. Teachers often are protective of girls and physically repressive of boys. Yet many boys are more emotionally fragile than we have realized, their brains and psyches slower to develop than girls' or more aggressive boys.' It is important to pay special attention to the more sensitive, less competitive, and less aggressive boys.

Preschool teachers need to understand the differences between boys' and girls' brains and the possible behavioral effects, as well as how to handle aggression in the preschool classroom.

INCREASING EMPATHY NURTURANCE AND VERBALIZATION   Young girls tend toward complex verbal nurturance strategies (boys are up to a year behind in verbal skills), and boys tend toward complex physical nurturance strategies, yet there are girls who practice aggression nurturance better than boys, and boys who seek empathy nurturance more than girls. Each gender tends to be pulled toward mass behavior, and boys and girls who don't fit the typical interactive hierarchies feel left out. Preschool and kindergarten are frightening for such children, and they can suffer emotional harm. To prevent this, we must teach young children to use other nurturance styles and increase children's use of words, especially words that explain feelings. We say to an aggressive child, "Use your words," to redirect aggression nurturance toward empathy nurturance.

➡ *Using Your Words:* One preschool teacher observed that a boy's aggressive behavior often followed a verbally aggressive act by a girl (calling him "stupid"). The teacher's solution was one-on-one conversation with the boy and the girl, in which she redirected both of their behaviors (helping the boy to make a connection between the external stimulant, his feelings, and his physical behavior). A preschool child who was being taught to use concrete words instead of actions to display emotions told another child, "I don't like it when you hit me. Please stop." Then he told his teacher what he had said and was very proud of himself.

"Using your words" is valuable in increasing neural connections between the upper brain and middle brain and between the left hemisphere and the limbic system. Boys and girls benefit from it, with male brains gaining neural connections they make less naturally than do females, and females gaining a less physically aggressive, verbally safer environment that fits their natural brain development.

Teachers need to mentor both aggression and empathy. Rules against cruelty must be a central component of all preschools. Children who are not directed to follow them are not well enough bonded with caregivers or experiencing appropriate discipline and mentoring. On the other hand, rules against all aggression show a teacher's lack of ability to fully bond, discipline, and mentor—especially the boys. Rather than learning life lessons through natural aggression, children learn that aggression is too difficult to manage in society and must be shut down. Because these children will practice their aggression somewhere else, where adult supervision may not exist, they may learn that it is only adults who fear it. It is essential to notice that nurturance and learning take place when it appears that children are being tough on each other.

➡ *Healthy Aggression Play:* At a minimum, the playground can become an area for healthy aggression fantasy play, like shadow karate kicks.

➡ *Discussing Aggression:* Teachers can train students to understand what aggression is, where it comes from, and how to turn it into purpose and service to others.

➡ *Healthy Competition:* Encourage healthy competitive learning so that girls do not end up disadvantaged compared to boys, who may naturally seek competitive activities in other parts of life.

DISCIPLINE TECHNIQUES Brain research suggests innovations in discipline. Generally, there is more need to go beyond words toward other solutions in disciplining boys, as they constitute 80 to 90 percent of preschool and kindergarten discipline problems.

Our research indicates that the presence of elders, parent volunteers, and even teen volunteers calms down a classroom and has a positive effect on children's behavior.

The following techniques can work in nearly any preschool and kindergarten:

➡ *Establish Cause-and-Effect:* Show the child the effect of an inappropriate action. Direct his eyes to the bruise or other damage his behavior caused.

➡ *Create Safe Outlets:* Put a Nerf bat and cushion in an "angry place" corner of the room as a safe place for a child to redirect hitting energy from animate to inanimate objects. Teach the child that he should not hit a living thing in anger.

➡ *Be Consistent and Firm:* When asking for an action to desist, say "please" once, maybe twice, but then become stern.

➡ *Use Time-Outs:* Give the child a time-out as necessary, and encourage the teacher or other angry adult to take one as needed.

➡ *Refuse to Engage in Power Struggles:* Ignore a child's refusal; don't engage in a power struggle. Allow sixty seconds for the child to begin to do what you ask. If defiance persists, institute other techniques.

➡ *Negotiate and Offer Two Choices:* Negotiate as much as is appropriate and offer choices (usually just two, for example, "You may put the block here or over there; which do you choose?").

➡ *Divert and Distract:* When possible, rely on diverting or distracting rather than punishing.

➡ *Take Away Privileges:* Take away privileges and toys as punishment.

➡ *Use Positive Words:* Present expectations in positive language (for example, "Isn't it great how we expect you to carry those plants inside today? How important you get to be").

➡ *Use "Games":* Make things into games whenever possible (for example, "Let's see how fast you can get your coat on. Look, I'm timing you!").

➡ *Be Specific:* Identify the specific challenge of a task or expectation. Point the child to it and help him focus on it, to reduce failure and the need for punishment.

➡ *Allow Mistakes:* Allow mistakes and failures; use them as teaching tools.

Discipline systems are often the result of adult dislike of a behavior, such as fidgeting. Understimulated, bored kids wiggle—the brain's reaction to an environment that is inappropriate for a child's energy level and neural skills. Girls are more able to self-manage boredom, while boys tend to turn boredom into impulsivity and acting out.

Bossiness also annoys teachers. We must help kids control their bossiness, but we don't want to overreact. Researchers at the University of California, Berkeley, discovered the link between bossiness (which boys tend to do physically and girls verbally) and better health. Less-dominant preschoolers have high heart rates and significant secretion of stress hormones. More-dominant preschoolers experience low heart rates and stress hormone secretion; their neural and central nervous systems are under less stress. For dominant and timid children alike, an ordered environment is helpful.

Elementary School

Many of today's children are not taught to respect elders, including teachers, and fear of punishment has diminished. A teacher's ability to create a well-disciplined classroom depends a great deal on how well she is bonded to her students.

Learning from Past Mistakes

Brain-based and gender-based training show that the following disciplinary measures are *counter*productive:

- *Exacting time-out during recess.* This often creates problems later in the day because a child was unable to expend physical energy.
- *Trying to force a confession or immediate self-assessment from an offending student.* The male brain is often slower at processing important emotive material, so boys cannot talk about what has happened as quickly and accurately as teachers often want them to.
- *Embarrassing the offender in front of classmates.* It can be effective, at times, to confront an offending student in front of classmates, but this should not be overdone and can be counterproductive. If the child's pride is hurt too much, the rest of the child's learning experience for that day, or longer, is ill-affected.

Most discipline problems in elementary school involve boys. Many female teachers are learning to accommodate normal boyish behavior. Much of it does not require discipline.

➡ *Expressing Disappointment in Behavior:* A second-grader shaped his hand like a gun and pretended to shoot the teacher, Claire. She privately told him how disappointed she was in his behavior and left it at that, as the boy had not crossed the line between aggression and violence. It is important not to overreact in such situations and not to let them interfere with the bonding relationship. If the child is expressing his nature rather than offending on purpose, expression of disappointment is enough and no other discipline is required.

Teachers want authority in the classroom, yet with each student feeling free to express the growing self. Walking the line between allowing student expression and retaining authority is the challenge of all discipline systems. There are standards for when to do more than just express alarm or disappointment about an aggressive gesture:

- If the student is, by use of the gesture, "dissing" the teacher in a way that inappropriately challenges teacher authority
- If the student has a history of violent or overly aggressive behavior
- If the aggressive gestures disrupt the class

Discipline Techniques After an Offending Act

As 90 percent of the discipline problems in schools are with boys, many discipline techniques are developed to fit male brains and behaviors. These techniques also work with girls, although there is less need for a long cool-down period with girls. Girls also tend to be quick at clearly verbalizing problems and are not so reliant on imposed authority. However, there is a great need to encourage a girl's ability to give voice to her own agendas and feelings. A combination of efforts generally helps return the child to self-discipline and the classroom to stability. Here are some techniques any teacher can use:

➡ *The Five-Step System:* At Balboa Elementary School, five steps are followed once an offending act has been committed. Depending on the severity of the act, the teacher may never need to go beyond step one.

1. *Teacher-Student Contact.* The teacher talks to or otherwise works with the offender, without outside help.
2. *Teacher-Parent Contact.* The teacher makes two attempts to contact parents. If she can't reach the parents, the head office keeps trying.
3. *Notifying the Principal.* The child sees the principal, or the principal otherwise becomes involved.
4. *Teacher–Support Personnel Contact.* This usually calls for a counselor or school psychologist, but it may be another teacher or a coach with whom the child is bonded.
5. *Excluding the Student.* If necessary, the child is excluded from the class. All previous steps are documented before resorting to this one.

➡ *Questions and Answers:* When offending children are sent to acting principal Jan Miller, she presents them with paper and pencils. They are to write responses to questions that help them work their way through their problems. The first question is usually "Why are you here?" This technique gives boys more time to think about their responses and, because they do not want to write any more than they have to, they select their words carefully. The technique also works well for girls, who ordinarily write more words and have less difficulty writing than boys do.

➡ *Nonconfrontational Techniques:* Carrie Whalley has noticed that boys find it difficult to open up when cornered or when a teacher says, "Look at me, I'm talking to you. What is wrong?" She tries to get something (crayons, blocks, cards) in the boy's hands while she's talking. Letting the child lower his head and move slowly, if needed, also helps to relax him and prevents a lot of frustration on both sides.

➡ *The Timer:* It is helpful to let time pass before expecting clarity from children who require discipline, especially boys, who generally need time to collect themselves enough to talk. When a child is angry, Carrie may set a timer for five minutes and tell the student that she will talk to him when the timer goes off. By the end of five minutes, they are both calm enough to talk. The cool-down period lets the brain prepare to process the emotion surrounding an action.

➡ *Buddy Rooms:* Students who do not respond well to a teacher's discipline are sent, in Denise Young's school, to a buddy room. This is a safe place to work out their problems. The buddy room can be the room of another teacher who has good rapport with, and the respect of, the students. When a sixth-grader refused to go to Denise's room when directed there by his classroom teacher, Denise took him aside and told him, "If you ever fail to respond to your teacher like that again, I will come get you and take you home." She foresees no further problem with him. Using a buddy room can backfire if the teacher is not bonded with the student she mentors; the offender can end up causing trouble in two classrooms rather than one.

➡ *Run an Errand:* At Jan Miller's school, when a child needs some time to get it together after creating a disturbance, he or she is given a card that states, "I need the Love and Logic book." There is no Love and Logic book. The child is sent on an errand to anyone to get it; that person sends the child to someone else, and ultimately back to the original class. By that time the child has cooled down and is ready to settle into class.

➡ *One-on-One Mentoring:* Alison Jabosky, a parent liaison, says her best discipline method is one-on-one mentoring that provides structure, attention, and positive reinforcement. Boys and girls both need this, but undisci-

plined boys seem to need ongoing mentoring most. Males often take longer to process the emotional and social material that goes into restabilizing themselves. Sometimes, only one-on-one mentoring can build enough trust for a breakthrough revelation to occur.

➡ *The BIST (Behavior Instruction Support Team) Model:* The BIST model was developed by the staff of the Ozanam School in the Kansas City, Missouri, area and is marketed to other school districts. The primary support for school personnel is a consultant who helps them when they have issues they can't resolve with students. BIST uses a "recovery room" for major offenses (for example, throwing a chair, cursing at a teacher, hitting another student). In some cases, the BIST system can result in substantial time out of class. However, it also results in fewer suspensions and expulsions as the students get older. It teaches students responsibility and self-control.

In one school, a disruptive student remains in the recovery room until he or she owns up to responsibility for the problem. This means the student may be there for more than one school day. Once the student is ready to accept responsibility, he or she "checks out" with the teacher at the teacher's convenience. The offense is processed, and a commitment is made to improve behavior. If the student does not comply with the direction to report to a specific room following an offense, the teacher notifies the Crisis Response Team (CRT)—a group of trained teachers—over the intercom (for example, "CRT to room 101"). Once the CRT arrives, all other students are taken out of the room. The CRT works with the disobedient student, physically removing the student if necessary. Students typically become obedient as soon as the CRT is involved because it is embarrassing to them to be carried down the hallway. Usually, an offending student chooses to go to the recovery room.

➡ *Peer Discipline:* Having students participate in school discipline systems helps to build responsibility. Such systems include hall monitors, peer-review boards, and student courtrooms. Students' input is considered in setting policies and procedures for such systems.

Techniques to Prevent Undisciplined Behavior

➡ *Task-Transition Warning:* Kimberly Walter says that her first-graders transition better from task to task, and require less reprimand, if she gives them forewarning. About three minutes prior to a transition, she announces that they have a few minutes to finish up, as well as what they will be doing next. Without this preparation time, boys especially are not ready to move on, and she wastes time getting into discipline situations with them. Males tend to have difficulty in multitasking and switching from one task to another quickly. The female brain is doing any given activity in more parts of the brain than the male and thus overlaps between activities more easily.

➡ *Acting and Rhyming:* When Rita Rome gives clean-up directions to kindergartners and first-graders, rather than giving a list, she has them act out everything as Rita demonstrates step-by-step (for example, picking up paint brushes, holding them in the air, putting them on the newspaper . . . show me how you rinse your hands under the water, show me how to get the soap) while reciting a poem about the process. She started this when a special-needs girl threw a tantrum because clean-up interrupted her art making. The acting out and rhyming holds the students' attention and helps them remember what to do.

➡ *Clapping:* Rita often needs to interrupt the students while they are working and talking. She uses the "clapping game." The teacher claps a pattern, and some hear it. Those students mimic the clapping pattern immediately. All the students hear that, and then the teacher does another pattern. All students should mimic the second round. They know that clapping means mimic, then stop, look, and listen. The announcement that follows can be spoken softly, as the clapping draws the students' attention.

➡ *Buddy Rooms:* Kimberly uses the buddy-room preventive technique. If she is going to be out one day and a substitute must take her class, to prevent a problem with a particularly difficult child, she arranges for him to spend that day in the class of a teacher with whom he works well. Nothing is gained by leaving a student in what will be for him, and may cause for others, a difficult situation.

➡ *Fewer Second Chances:* Teachers and parents often diminish their authority by granting a second chance. The adult does not realize that one of the best ways to maintain discipline is to use the child's sense that the adult is an alpha—a powerful leader. This sense is thwarted if the child has a number of second chances, especially in the late elementary and middle school years. Although a zero-tolerance policy generally erases good bonding and often does more harm than intended, allowing a thing to repeat multiple times does great harm to the whole learning environment. It is better to say, "Dana, if you do that again, you will lose your [whatever is appropriate] privilege." If the behavior is repeated, the child must face the consequence.

➡ *Pull Cards:* It is difficult to assess the accuracy of students who report misbehaviors. To help students take responsibility for their actions, one class suggested keeping a tally of offenses on "pull cards." The students can physically see how many violations they have and what their limits are. The class tallies violations; once a child is over the limit, he or she is sent to the principal. The method works well, the class is stabilizing, and new discipline problems are preempted.

Conflict and Anger Management

➡ *Identifying Feelings:* Helping children to identify and act out their feelings not only helps to defuse them but also helps the children learn to recognize differences so that they do not always react in the same ways (such as crying or hitting). For example, children can be asked to describe anger (and how it differs from resentment), boredom, sadness, envy, happiness (what makes them happy), and so on. They also can be asked to make faces depicting different emotions and to describe other students' emotions based on the faces that the other students are making. This can help them to develop more skill in "reading" others' moods.

➡ *Helping Children Verbalize Their Feelings:* When a boy, especially, becomes upset, learning is put on hold. Rita Rome pulls the child aside, has him label what he is feeling, validates those feelings, and helps him get past it ("Are you feeling angry? That's okay; I would be angry too!") Once he sees that someone understands and accepts his anger, he is more likely to deal with it.

➡ *Cool-Down Time:* Rita allows students to leave the group and cool down without feeling punished.

➡ *Teaching Children to Solve Their Own Problems:* Children can be taught to use "I" statements to express their feelings. In conflict situations, this involves describing the other person's behavior or the problem and how it affects them (without accusing or blaming). They can practice doing this with basic ground rules, such as "make eye contact" and "no interrupting." Children can learn to methodically work through identified problems and conflicts by brainstorming possible solutions, examining them, and agreeing on the most workable solution.

➡ *Pantomime:* To avoid class disruption, Rita teaches her students to pantomime to one another to convey messages. For example, if a boy returns to the group in the middle of a lesson, sees another student in his chair, and starts a confrontation (physically moving the "invader"), Rita calls a break and acts out how to say, "Excuse me," without touching or speaking. The students act it out. Then the class acts out "May I have my seat?" The students discover how easy it is to communicate without disrupting the class.

➡ *Switching Sides:* In a form of role playing, children are asked to take another's "side" and argue as if they were the other. This expands their views of an issue. It often leads to parody and giggles, which also help to diffuse the conflict.

➡ *Assigning Group Responsibility:* Toward the end of the year, students sometimes begin bickering on the playground (usually girls). When it first occurs, Carol Meyers brings all the students involved together and places their names in a container. She tells them that it is too difficult to decide which ones are having the problem (girls tend to change "best friends" frequently), so the next time a problem occurs between any of them, she will simply pull three names out of the container and those three will receive the consequence. This has taken care of the petty bickering; it also keeps Carol from being the bad guy because the names in the container are predetermined, and she lets a student draw the names.

➡ *Peer Mediation:* In some cases, a peer mediator, a peer panel, or the entire class can be asked to resolve a conflict or solve a problem. The problem is summarized (by both sides, if they exist). Sometimes, opposing sides are asked to state the other's point of view. The mediator, teacher, or a panel member then summarizes what has been said and asks for any other pertinent information. Opposing sides (if they exist) or the panel or class members are asked to suggest possible solutions. These are discussed in terms of workability, possible consequences, and so on. The sides may be instructed to select a solution, or the class may vote. Trained older students can be brought in to serve as mediators. They do not assign solutions but help the younger children to work through the problem-solving process.

Motivational Techniques

Between 70 and 80 percent of students with motivation problems are boys. Teachers have had to seek male-brain solutions to motivational problems, although many of these techniques also can work with girls.

➡ *Time Limits:* Carrie Whalley challenges unmotivated students to do something in a certain amount of time (for example, "Let's see if you can do these three math problems in two minutes").

➡ *Playing to Pride:* Rita Oglesby's school uses pride and embarrassment to motivate students, particularly boys, to take responsibility for their behavior. Undisciplined and unmotivated students are directed to primary grade teachers who have been there for a number of years and who have good rapport because of their consistent discipline. In part, because these are teachers whom the boys respect the most, the boys are embarrassed to be sent to them for messing up. They are also embarrassed to be in a primary grade classroom.

Character Education

Classroom issues such as discipline and motivation often can be resolved by practical strategies, but schools have even more success if character education is stressed throughout the schools. Unless grounded in "hard" values, such as respect, honesty, and integrity, "soft" values, such as self-esteem, easily can become paths to self-indulgence. Character development serves the growing moral needs of the child. Twenty-eight states either require or encourage character education.

Character education works best when it is integrated into all departments of a school and teachers receive training in how to integrate it. For instance, a science teacher might ask a class to analyze the ethics of a science project or might ask for a character analysis of certain scientists; a history teacher might help students trace how our civilization has or has not acted with "character."

➡ *CHARACTERplus:* A program called CHARACTERplus, developed in Missouri, is now used nationally and is compatible with brain-based research. The process starts with community members, including educators, who meet to identify and define the character traits they want their community's children to demonstrate. The process helps community members move from distrust of one another to mutual respect and commitment. Between communities, similarities tend to outnumber differences. For example, practically all communities agree on the character traits of honesty, respect, and responsibility.

Teachers are taught to integrate the traits into the existing curricula, and community members commit to supporting, modeling, and teaching them as well. One community's traits are as follows:

- *Respect:* showing positive regard for self, others, and property
- *Accountability:* willingness to be responsible for our actions and to accept the consequences of those actions
- *Empathy:* ability to relate to and understand the feelings of others
- *Responsibility:* being accountable for one's actions
- *Recognition of Diversity:* acknowledging differences and appreciating individuals as equal members of society
- *Honesty:* willingness to be truthful in both words and actions
- *Compassion:* carrying out action sympathetic to others in an effort to assist
- *Cooperation:* the action of working together for mutual benefit to accomplish a task
- *Self-Confidence:* positive belief in oneself and in one's ability
- *Resourcefulness:* creating ways to achieve positive solutions or outcomes

➡ *Character Matters:* This is a free program for grades three through twelve. It comes with a curriculum guide (cowritten by Dr. Edward DeRoche, co-director of the International Center for Character Education at the University of San Diego), offering a variety of strategies to help teachers (and parents) use newspaper content to teach values such as respect, honesty, fairness, compassion, and courage. The stages include the following and more:

- *Awareness and Concepts*: Students find and define value words by referring to newspapers, literature, storytelling, and real-life experiences; ask their parents and others about their views of the values; and find sayings about the values and display them in the classroom.
- *Analysis, Synthesis, Comprehension, and Evaluation*: Students find examples of a value in literature, history, and the newspaper; discuss the value and compare and contrast the examples; write a headline or draw a comic strip about the value; list questions about the value and find examples in the newspaper that help answer their questions; evaluate why some people demonstrate the value and some do not; and keep a scrapbook of newspaper content about the value and record their ideas and feelings about it.
- *Application-Action and Observation of Effects:* Students discuss how the values apply to their daily lives and how they could demonstrate use of the values, role play the values in class and have other students react to the role play, ask their parents how they see the values applied at work, keep a journal of observations of how the values are or are not applied in their peer group and on television, and write letters to the editor in response to newspaper items about the values.

Some of the educational strategies included are self-directed work; pair and group work; reading; writing; journaling; discussion; storytelling; acting; drawing comics and illustrating; research; interviewing parents, grandparents, and others; creating posters, bulletin boards, and collages; finding examples; and exploring symbolism.

In the related "Laws of Life" essay contest (developed by the John Templeton Foundation), students submit essays describing the rules, ideals, and principles by which they live and explain the sources (for example, literature, life experiences, religion, culture, role models) of their "laws." The contest is part of President Bush's "Friendship Through Education" consortium of nongovernmental organizations, including Newspaper in Education (NIE).

Dealing with Cruelty, Hazing, and Violence

The increase in teasing and humiliation behavior in our schools has been noticed by educators, parents, and the judicial system. This behavior can be a character issue. When does teasing become humiliation, and when does humiliation become illegal harassment? At what point do all of these behaviors become violence? While these questions are decided by the courts, the classroom must be safe and enjoy standards of behavior that are both realistic and enforceable.

DEFINITION OF TERMS The following definitions will be helpful for schools that are deciding on policies regarding teasing, harassment, hazing, and related behaviors:

- *Teasing.* Teasing is a normal activity in which children focus on real or perceived weaknesses in peers. Especially in elementary school, friendships are just as frequently cemented by teasing as they are destroyed. Teasing is a way of one-upping but also is often flirtatious. It exists in human relations as a means of building strength in a peer community. Most children adapt to it and grow stronger from the process. Some, especially those who are less confident, are harmed by it.
- *Humiliation.* Humiliation is also a normal activity among peers, but it is generally practiced by children who are perceived (or who perceive themselves) to be at the upper end of a hierarchy. These children generally pick a variety of targets.
- *Harassment.* Harassment is repeated targeting of one or more individuals, over a prolonged period, which generally uses one or more psychosocial traits (for example, physical features, race, sexual identity, gender, social class, intellectual disability, emotional vulnerability) as the basis for the harassment.

Teasing and humiliation are generally normal—although painful—forms of human aggression, practiced by both boys and girls in gender-specific ways. But harassment is generally a form of violence and can escalate into physical assault.

- *Aggression and Violence.* Aggression is an individual's attempt to control or manipulate another person or system. This is normal human behavior. Violence is an individual's attempt to destroy the core self or existence of another individual or system. This destruction can be accomplished on a behavioral spectrum that runs from incessant shaming to physical attack and, in the extreme, systematic annihilation.

➡ *Responding to Teasing:* Children can be taught to deal with teasing and other unwanted behaviors assertively and with nondefensive communication. The following are suggested steps:

1. Ignore the other child.
2. Move away from the other child.
3. Politely ask the other child to stop the behavior. State the effect on you (for example, "When you _____, I feel _____. I would appreciate it if you would _____").
4. Speak firmly, without raising your voice.
5. If these steps don't work, ask an adult to help.

ZERO-TOLERANCE POLICIES AND OTHER MEASURES Boys and girls experience aggression differently. Zero-tolerance policies are useful but often are too rigid and inhumane. They are easier to support in small, private schools with small classroom size, more bonding and mentoring, more one-on-one attention to students, and a narrower student behavioral range. If a school is set up to prevent student unruliness by providing constant supervision, zero tolerance is compatible with the structure experienced by the students. If many students in a large school do not get the mentoring and bonding they need, zero-tolerance policies are—like Ritalin and other medication—often evidence of how overwhelmed the school is, not how humane.

The exception is zero tolerance of actual violence and of gang attire or activity. Gang involvement is an example of students seeking bonding opportunities in isolationist, violence-based systems rather than in school systems; in this case, zero tolerance is essential.

➡ *Violence-Prevention Training:* In tandem with character education, violence-prevention training is essential for teachers, staff members, and students. Much school violence is preventable—not necessarily by teachers, but by students, some of whom are intimate with potential offenders. As students are trained in community responsibility and learn the options open to them, they are forthcoming, motivated by empathy for a troubled classmate and a sense of responsibility for the whole school.

➡ *Harassment Rules:* It is essential that each school promulgate and post harassment rules. Such rules are most effective when combined with student training in such terms as "aggression," "teasing," and "harassment." Following the posting, enforcement policies—appropriate to the school and its legislative mandates—should also be declared. The following are sample rules:

- A student or group of students may not repeatedly taunt another student
- A student or group of students may not hit another student
- Students who witness harassment or violence must report it

➡ *Honor Training:* Honor training and honor codes should be considered by all schools. If possible, all students should be involved in designing and then signing the honor code.

➡ *Nonbullying Curricula:* There are many training programs available to aid communities in stopping violent behavior. One is "On Target to Stop Bullying," which is marketed by the Stop Violence Coalition in Kansas City, Missouri. It uses principles consistent with brain and biological information in violence prevention.

Another program is Act-React®, which is designed to challenge kids to think and reason about consequences and to discover values for themselves. There are versions of the program for grade school through high school.

Whatever program a school uses, it is essential that all teachers be trained in a stop-bullying curriculum rooted in understanding of how boys and girls actually think and feel. Programs of this kind teach skills for handling misbehavior and edify teachers about their students' confusing behaviors.

The Role of Media

The effects of media influence, especially on male violence, must be dealt with by every school district. According to media literacy expert John Caputo, "Acts of violence exceed eleven per hour on evening TV. By the end of high school, the average student has spent 11,000 hours in the classroom, watched 15,000 hours of television, listened to 10,500 hours of popular music, seen 350,000 commercials, and witnessed 18,000 media deaths."

The human brain is affected by these images in problematic ways. Teachers and parents need training in media literacy and responsibility. Many children are allowed at home to surf the Internet inappropriately, watch whatever television they want, and see developmentally inappropriate movies. Through parent-education coordinators, schools can educate parents in good standards for media use.

→ *What Stories Does My Son Need?:* This book, by Michael Gurian and Terry Trueman, lists one hundred books and one hundred movies that build character in children. It is one attempt to link media literacy to character development.

→ *Pokemon:* Japanese elementary schools use this value-based game to instill empathy, responsibility, and cooperation in students. Students can be asked for reports on what the characters mean and how they help one another to succeed.

Middle School

Middle school discipline is particular. Students, particularly boys, are loud, and students often have difficulty sitting still. There also are individual discipline issues. Kids who have problems at home often act out (for example, by seeking attention or roughhousing); some may have trouble paying attention because of inadequate sleep or nutrition.

Strategies for Providing Discipline

We need to understand how much bonding the most behaviorally deficient kids need in order to improve.

→ *Consistency:* Carry out consistently applied discipline systems in all classes, with teachers and administrators working as a discipline team, rather than as isolated authorities.

➡ *Discipline Plan:* Lilly Figueroa's school has a discipline plan that all students are given instruction in. They all know the consequences of their actions, regardless of what class they are in.

➡ *Classroom Rules:* Lilly has her classroom rules posted, and a copy is given to each student. Consequences are equal for all students. Although they might not be happy with a consequence, they know it is fair. She has students help her define the rules and consequences at the beginning of the school year; in this way, they buy into the classroom-management plan.

➡ *Student-Adult Groups:* In Lilly's former school, all students were divided into groups, three times a week, for one-half hour, for the entire time they were in the school. Groups were small, so teachers knew each student's likes and dislikes. Every adult in the school was involved; they discussed students, talked about problems, and found solutions to some problems. With each student, they wrote letters, played games, and formed a tight bond. A student who had a problem had an adult he or she could look up to and feel confident going to.

➡ *Tension-Release Strategies:* Provide students (especially boys) with quick tension-release strategies, both within and outside the classroom. Examples are stress balls and foam Nerf bats with harmless targets.

➡ *The BIST (Behavior Instruction Support Team) Model:* This model (introduced in the "elementary school" section of this chapter) is also used in middle school. Brandy Barnett describes a male student who became angry and flipped a desk over, striking her foot. It was a typical male reaction—immediate and explosive without thinking. The student immediately felt terrible about it, shut himself in the recovery room, and wouldn't come out for two hours, until his mother came. When he came back to school after his suspension, Brandy made sure that she let him and everyone else know that she still cared about him.

➡ *Saturday Detention Chores:* One teacher has a Saturday detention schedule, taking students into the school yard to rake leaves or into the community to do other chores. He reports that the kids enjoy it because they're getting love and attention that they don't get at home, especially as most of them have no fathers.

➡   *When in Doubt, Become an Alpha:* Young male elephants that had been brought up without parents in Africa began killing rhinoceroses (very unusual behavior) and trying to mate inappropriately. They were following their hormonal urges without guidance from elders or alpha role models. Alpha male elephants were brought in from another part of Africa and, within a week, the inappropriate behaviors ceased.

When faced with a student who is trying to dominate and destroy, sometimes there is no recourse but to become an alpha: strict, no second chances, rapport based on strong authority. If you can't do it, enlist the aid of a potential alpha you know.

➡   *Antibullying Campaigns:* Formal antibullying and safe-school campaigns are necessary in many districts. "On Target to Stop Bullying," a program guide for addressing bullying and violence in schools, is a project of the STOP Violence Coalition and the Missouri Safe Schools Coalition. The Act-React program also helps teachers to facilitate discussions that challenge youths to think about the consequences of their aggressive actions.

➡   *Journaling:* Ruth Whertvine has her students keep journals, and those with greater discipline issues sometimes write about their issues. Occasionally, Ruth asks her students to participate in their own emotional education by writing on an emotion-based theme, such as "feeling frustrated" (that is, when did they feel it and what did they do about it?). Boys tended to report doing physical activities rather than trying to talk it out.

➡   *The Sixty-Second Rule:* Ruth tells students what to do and gives them sixty seconds to do it. If they start to question and argue, she goes on to something else. They almost always do what they have been told to do if they cannot engage her in a verbal battle and the focus of the classroom is not on them.

Middle school boys are generally involved in psychological separation from their mothers and caught up in battles of pride and hierarchy with classmates. Allowing sixty seconds for compliance, and turning away from a conflict, can stave off a lot of misbehavior.

➡ *The Boys Town Social-Skills Model:* Number five of the Boys Town Classroom Social Skills is getting the teacher's attention: (1) Look at the teacher; (2) raise your hand, stay calm; (3) wait until the teacher says your name; (4) ask your question.

➡ *Separate-Sex Groupings:* Especially in middle school, this has the potential to decrease discipline problems. Even if they are not separated in class, boys and girls can be separated in the lunchroom, during study hall, and during in-school suspension. Both boys and girls accomplish more when they are not showing off for or distracted by the presence of the other sex.

Community Collaboration

➡ *Community Collaboration:* Brenda Bock believes that there is a direct relationship between chores and responsibilities carried out at home and discipline and completion of work at school. Community collaboration in the area of discipline is crucial. A parent-education coordinator can teach parents effective discipline techniques.

➡ *Mentoring:* Some school districts bring fathers into schools as volunteers. Strong mentors often are needed for minority and at-risk males. Some mentors come from the Big Brothers Big Sisters of America's school-based mentoring program. Some are elder volunteers. College students can be coached to mentor high school students, who can mentor middle schoolers. Discipline problems on a school bus can be helped by having a grandfather ride on the bus. (See more on this topic in the section on mentoring.)

Character Education

The advantage of consistent discipline to children is clear, as is development of a strong core self. A hidden by-product of character education (see description in "elementary school" section) is its ability to improve academic learning. A student who feels strong in character is better motivated to perform well when the going gets tough, as it always does at some point. In middle school, children benefit from having character education absorbed into all classes.

➡ *Comparing Definitions:* Pay attention to what each gender might mean by good character and how this might be similar to or different from what the other gender means by it.

➡ *CHARACTERplus:* This model (described previously) is useful in middle school and beyond. Although the definitions of desired traits vary with the community, the similarities are greater than the differences.

➡ *VIP Program:* The staff at Smith-Hale Middle School asked students what they would most like to be able to do while attending school. The most common responses were (1) go to the restroom without getting a hall pass, (2) visit the vending machines after lunch periods, and (3) wear badges like the adults do. The staff linked this information to the school's character-education program. Students who exhibit good citizenship or character are selected as VIPs. Once selected, they remain VIPs unless they lose their badges (for three infractions of any character trait).

➡ *Extending Character Education to Other Aspects of School Life:* At Smith-Hale, staff members now consistently model the character traits, and parents are encouraged to reinforce the character traits. The parents asked that the traits be included in the student handbook so they would have easy access to them.

➡ *Service Learning:* A fast-growing initiative in schools is service learning, an approach that moves beyond the concept of community service to a higher, more academically integrated type of instructional practice. No longer is community service done at the expense of academic instruction. Service learning integrates academic curriculum with a strong character-education component. Students take responsibility to choose topics, develop plans, and engage in meaningful community action. *Service Learning: Curriculum, Standards and the Community,* a video published by Phi Delta Kappa International, visits programs in New York and Missouri as teachers develop service-learning projects with their secondary students that promote academic, social, and civic responsibility.

High School

Lack of discipline causes immense stress for high school teachers and students. Teacher-student and peer bonds can be built or broken by discipline issues. High school is similar to middle school in this way, although there generally is more maturity and a somewhat less serious breakdown of discipline. However, high-risk behavior has always been high among adolescent males and is increasing among adolescent girls. Both want the community to impose limits; the high school student's brain craves discipline as much as it craves free individual expression.

Discipline of high school students is a crucial, holistic process of adulthood maturation. High school is the last chance to develop the limits and self-management (self-discipline) the mind needs to succeed in the adult world.

Techniques to Prevent Undisciplined Behavior

Much of what we've said about earlier school years is applicable to high school discipline. High school students need

- A firm and loving teacher, who genuinely cares about each student and shows it
- A teacher who sets strict rules and reinforces them verbally and nonverbally
- A teacher who sets high expectations and helps each student rise to meet them
- A classroom environment that provides equal educational and technological opportunities to every student
- A team-learning environment in which students' emotional stress management is an integral part of the learning process
- Openness to discipline innovations—as opposed to a single set of strategies that may not work in some cases
- Support from other teachers and administrators for giving help to problem students
- Conflict-resolution standards and practices that take precedence over academic learning
- Access to alternative education when a student needs it
- Consistent support for discipline from home and family
- A school-wide character-education program
- Mandatory service programs

➡ *Encourage Teacher Authority:* Especially in dealing with boys, teachers should carry powerful authority, whether in personal charisma or in consistency, academic quality, and intuition of teenagers' needs.

➡ *Discipline Councils:* Healthy brain development requires clear and well-enforced discipline. Peer mediation, peer conflict resolution, and peer discipline councils help high school students take more responsibility for self-discipline while adults supervise and teach methodology.

As instituted by St. Mark's School, discipline councils of ten or more students and three or more teachers (and sometimes an administrator and/or parent representative) are part of the school discipline system. Offenses in school are rated according to severity. Level-one offenses are corrected on the spot by a teacher. Level-two offenses may go to the vice principal or another disciplinarian. Level-three offenses (such as hazing, vandalism, cheating, repeated failure to attend class, and recurrent defiance of authority) go before the council. The behavior of the student and of all the people involved in the incident—including teachers—is scrutinized. Generally, the student is required by a vote of peers to make redress and is sometimes suspended. Occasionally, a teacher's behavior is found wanting.

→ *Talking About Problems:* Hold check-in and talk time in human growth and development, social studies, psychology, and other applicable classes, in which students have a chance to verbalize issues they face, including harassment, depression, and bullying.

→ *Maximize "Teachable" Moments:* Janet Rodgers has found that some students and groups of students lack moral "literacy" or compasses; at times, they need deliberate guidance. This became apparent when a student in her computer-education class was caught copying computer files from another. Most class members thought this was a trivial thing. When Janet made the connection between copying files and stealing items from someone's locker, students began to realize the gravity of the infraction, and a useful discussion ensued.

Character Education and Service Projects

As students approach adulthood, character-education efforts continue to be important. St. Augustine's High School, in San Diego, has forty-eight rules in its handbook, random drug testing every eight to ten days, and one hundred hours of mandatory community service a year. Students at St. Augustine's generally give these measures positive feedback.

→ *Mandatory Service Projects:* Many schools require some form of school or community service (for example, volunteering in and visiting people in nursing homes, doing community cleanup) as a prerequisite for graduation from high school. Although some students perform the service only because it is required, it still teaches the reluctant. We highly recommend mandatory service hours for all high school students for all years.

→ *Antibullying Campaigns:* The two programs mentioned earlier, "On Target to Stop Bullying" and Act-React, help teachers help teens to grow toward being responsible citizens.

Helping Young Males to Manage Aggression

Many high school males try to be tough and defiant to try to "fit in." Brain-based research reveals the natural internal conflict between high levels of male aggression and the need to develop self-management of that aggression.

➡ *Peer Mediation:* When conflicts emerge between students, peer mediation is very useful. This is a mentored program in which students are selected and trained to become mediators in other students' conflicts. Girls often use highly verbal strategies, and boys use few words, but the outcome is equally powerful for both.

Training males who exhibit a need for dominance in peer mediation helps them learn to balance the abilities in the top of the brain (facilitating safety and relational harmony to promote the self) with those in the middle and lower brain (use of aggression and ego to promote the self). Such students learn to use their conflict-resolution skills in other settings.

Toledo, Ohio, Catholic high schools practice a six-step peer-mediation process. The students go into middle schools and train sixth- through eighth-graders in peer mediation. While training the younger students, they mediate middle school conflicts. The middle schoolers, in turn, gain training to help mediate conflicts among younger children. Through the feeder-school interactions, early bonds form that carry through later grades.

Math, Science, and Spatial Learning

TEACHERS WILL FIND CERTAIN TECHNIQUES AND APPROACHES IN THIS CHAPTER THAT pertain to any grade level. These include

1. Varying the teaching media and modalities (for example, using manipulatives; movement; the physical environment; and puzzles, problem-solving activities, and learning games
2. Teaching to all the senses (using visual, auditory, and kinesthetic input and assigning visual, auditory, and kinesthetic tasks)
3. Using same-gender and mixed-gender learning groups

Preschool and Kindergarten

The following suggestions are based on research into how boys and girls learn best.

Techniques to Encourage Learning

➡ *Reduce Verbal Instructions:* To keep boys interested, keep verbal instructions to less than a minute before going into an activity.

➡ *Movement-Based Games:* Play kickball and other movement-based games to help girls learn gross motor skills (in which they are weaker than boys).

➡ *Puzzles:* Use lots of puzzles to help both boys and girls with perceptual learning.

➡ *Characters in Block Activities:* Kathi Winkler wanted to get girls more interested in a spatial-block activity, which was usually dominated by boys building high towers. She gave the girls "people" to relate to by asking the children to build small toy people (authentic in detail and sturdy enough to be handled and stand up), in the block area. It changed construction activities from using blocks to make the highest tower into cooperative building of settings for doctors, police officers, teachers, merchants, families, and so on. The "people" linked play and language to spatial learning and gave the girls more investment in block play because it included relationships. It also increased the girls' self-confidence in working in an area that boys were dominating.

Small, plastic, hotel shampoo and lotion bottles, filled with sand and with the tops securely glued on, are good bases for creating toy "people" for games and other activities.

➡ *Conflicts That Teach Problem Solving:* To get boys to solve problems tied to a math or spatial skill, Kathi gives choices that can create conflicts. The boys seem more willing to work on negotiation and intellectual skills when the problems are genuine and of interest to them. For example, each day a different child is selected to distribute snacks, on a rotating basis (this involves personal responsibility and managing group interaction). Kathi asks, "How many cookies do you think each child can have today?" The answer provides insights into the child's ideas of numbers, quantities, and part-whole relationships. Some children say "two" because that seems to be a usual number of cookies. Kathi accepts the decision unless another child objects, when a discussion follows (involving conflict, discussion, and problem solving). One child said, "They can have as many cookies as they are years old." He asked each child, "Are you three or four?" and gave each child three or four cookies. There was no protest until he came to Mike, who said, "Four." "You aren't four, because I'm bigger and I'm three." Mike insisted that he was four. He was the oldest child in the class but also the smallest and youngest-looking. The discussion became lively. Kathi confirmed that Mike was four, and the children learned for the first time that age is not directly related to size.

In this kind of situation, shy girls and boys learn through observation; dominant children practice learning in their way; and it is difficult for any child to remain disengaged. Boys like conflict and excitement in learning, and girls can do spatials better if they are related to a person.

➡ *Lineup:* Another way to teach the concept of age versus size (and social perception) is to do a lineup (continuum) by age and then compare size, or vice versa.

Self-Directed Activities

Brain research indicates that at least a third of the class day should be reserved for self-direction, and some children can support more than half a day. For the developing brain, self-direction has many advantages; in a supportive, well-led environment, the mind gravitates toward learning what it needs to learn in order to grow. If a classroom lets the brain explore, it moves in the neural motions required. This is particularly important in early childhood, because the social interactions that occur between peers and between children and adults during this time impact development tremendously. Language, intellectual challenge, and social/moral development in early childhood flourish with choice, movement, and activity.

Kathi Winkler notices that girls can maximize their potential in a more sedentary, language-oriented environment, and boys seem to grow best when they are active and setting up their own challenges. Self-directed activity works for both genders, but teachers may find it especially helpful for those boys and girls who are not learning as successfully in other ways.

Integrated Use of the Physical Environment

The younger brain is not capable of much abstraction or verbal ideation; it learns in the concrete world. It learns to make sense of the physical environment by working in it—decoding what it does not understand and manipulating objects into patterns it can understand.

⮕   *Structure Building:* Kathi's students worked together in the block area to build a structure approximately four feet tall, with an area of about fifty square feet. They were confronted with challenges of balance and decisions about the purpose of the structure and the use of blocks. Kathi merely helped to keep them safe and helped them negotiate with one another using words rather than violence. The result was a complex building that incorporated over a hundred blocks, cars, and play figures.

Group and paired activity was successful here. The children had to work in physical space in order to learn. The more the various parts of the brain made neural connections, the more learning was likely. This is the kind of spatial activity from which girls often are excluded, because they may not feel as comfortable in it and because a boy may seek to dominate the space. This is an opportunity to include girls while not damaging the spontaneous and gender-defined play of the male group.

➡ *Climbing:* Build lofts in the classroom with safe steps and encourage kids to climb up to the top and otherwise experience three-dimensional space.

➡ *Water Tables and Sand Tables:* Use a water table and a sand table to make "scientific" things experiential.

Games to Encourage Logical-Mathematical Thinking

Games can encourage logical-mathematical thinking. Games meet girls' need for social connectedness while challenging them to become players in problem-solving activities rather than passive learners. Kathi uses games that allow children of varying developmental levels to play together. She sets out these games to be chosen during the children's self-directed work period.

To encourage mathematical exploration and play, a game includes interesting manipulatives. Girls tend to choose games with pieces that are attractive to look at and handle, particularly those with realistic animal or people tokens or treasure-like qualities. A successful game also includes clear rules and objectives (payoffs), active involvement, and competition and/or cooperation, as well as allowing some open-ended choices and more than one strategy to be employed.

➡ *Using Games for Math:* With groups of no more than six students, Kathi uses lots of manipulatives and small game pieces. With a theme of transportation, the tasks of counting, sorting, and categorizing—and playing games with cars and trucks as the tokens—leads boys into using numbers effectively. The children may also count the objects in each category and compare group quantities.

Male brains tend to favor a spatial task as the challenge base of a learning experience. It is important to make sure that girls participate; they need it just as much or more. Such activities are best done in small groups, so that wait time is short and hands-on time is increased.

➡ *The Treasure Game:* This consists of individual game boards picturing ocean scenes and treasures, with a path to follow. The tokens are small plastic sailboats just large enough to collect small, brightly colored gems along the way. Each time a player lands on the treasure spot, she collects a gem and continues her move to deposit it into her cache.

Two five-year-old girls and a four-year-old boy in Kathi's class chose to play the Treasure Game together. Each child chose a game board and a favorite color of boat. They chose to use a large die as a move indicator, although they could have used a spinner or cards. The first problem was who would go first, and Kathi showed ways to negotiate a solution. One girl suggested that the three draw straws. As girls learn to use strategies such as drawing straws, paper-scissors-rock, and flipping coins, it moves them past the passive realm of gaining or being denied privileges based on gender.

Each child uses his or her own developmental level of counting. For example, one girl understood that two numbers could make up a larger number. As she rounded the board, she was able to split her roll in order to collect a treasure and then continue her move. This was confusing to the boy, who stopped his moves when he reached the treasure mark, regardless of the quantity he had rolled. He challenged the girl, insisting that she stop as he did and that she was cheating. Rather than giving in to his insistence that the game be played according to his understanding, the girl explained her reasoning. She physically showed how loading a boat was only a pause during the count instead of an end point. At this point, the game almost ended in contention, but she persuaded the other two to keep playing. Eventually, the others imitated her strategy. This move to higher-level thinking allowed all three to play more quickly and to collect more treasures.

This type of game provides girls an opportunity to think mathematically, to defend their understanding of number concepts, and to use social language to communicate mathematical understanding. Without challenges to their thinking, girls often get stuck in looking for the right answer rather than for multiple solutions that can be examined and defended.

➡ *Use of Physical Objects (Manipulatives):* Boys learn best when lessons are experiential, with lots of blocks and other manipulatives for play and lesson learning. Using manipulatives, such as number rolls, to teach mathematics compels students' brains to make the math concrete and particularly aids girls (and boys) who are not inherently talented in math calculation or design.

Kathi described a three-year-old boy who needed continual involvement in a sensory-motor activity to learn effectively. One week, he spent most of his time at the water table exploring pumps and boats, experimenting with things that sink and float. He made comparisons of the boats in the water table, including their sizes. He learned that a boat floats when empty but sinks when full of water. He discussed his point of view with another child as they took turns with the pump and sorted out the boats. He talked with Kathi and the other child about his explorations. He worked on colors and counting as he noticed the attributes of the boats. Although these skills could be taught in a teacher-directed group, his involvement probably would have been less enthusiastic if all his senses were not part of the activity.

Such innovations help to keep harder-to-handle and easily distracted boys involved in the learning process and excite their brains toward learning comfort. They also help girls expand their learning strengths beyond verbal skills into spatial competence.

Elementary School

The two areas of most pronounced difficulty—and the most copious brain and social research—in the elementary school are reading and writing, math and science. Gender- and brain-based innovations can help.

Techniques to Encourage Learning

➡ *Externalize Thought Processes About Math:* Jill Lamming helps students see how math and science work. She includes in lessons the strategies of outlining thought processes and self-questioning techniques. For example, to figure out the value of a number with a decimal, the first thing the student needs to ask is, "Is this a whole number?" The next step is to locate where the decimal falls in the number. Students are encouraged to do this outside their heads, by asking a question, writing the answer, or seeing it on a graph. Talking through and outlining processes on a chart helps girls to visualize and work through what might seem second nature to boys. Diagramming information also is a useful visual tool for girls.

➡ *Vary the Media:* Teach higher levels of math, not just on the board (which requires abstraction and favors male brains) but also with graphs, charts, and written material on paper, to help girls learn.

➡ *Even Out Computer Time:* Beginning around third grade or age nine, give girls special access to technology, computers, and the Internet, along with a little extra encouragement to use and master them. (Intense computer use before about age nine may be hazardous to brain development.)

Using Manipulatives Whenever Possible

Using real objects and manipulatives helps girls, especially, to learn math and science, subjects they do not "get" as naturally as boys do.

Stacy Moyer says that young children learn a lot from sorting and manipulating objects: counting, classifying, comparing and contrasting, and beginning addition and subtraction skills. They also work on visual discrimination, problem solving, and fine motor coordination. When encouraged to work with other children, they learn from one another and enhance their communication skills.

➡ *Using Beans/Pasta/Buttons:* Stacy finds that kids love to manipulate beans (and different shapes of dry pasta, buttons, and other materials). She buys a variety of dried beans and provides ice cube trays for sorting. The kids sort the beans by size, color, or shape.

➡ *Blocks for Girls:* To encourage girls in using blocks, Monica Miller uses Lego® pieces that build castles, houses, and barns and are geared toward girls (most boys already like to use Lego blocks). Monica encourages all the children to create verbal story lines to go along with the homes and towns they build. This helps their language development and social skills.

➡ *Time and Money:* In teaching third-graders about clocks and money, Jan Miller gives her students clocks with movable hands and some bags of change. Throughout the day, she calls for time checks or money checks. Students must write down the correct time or count their money. This quick activity also helps to break up the day.

➡ *Coins:* Denise Young has done a similar activity. Periodically, she puts certain coins on the board. Students must count them and record the correct amount. At the end of the week, they turn in their answers for an extra recess or a special time to read.

➡ *Magnets:* Denise also did a magnet unit with a lot of hands-on activities. The testing of the different objects made a real difference in the level of understanding. The movement keeps the boys' interest.

➡ *Venn Diagram:* In a fourth-grade class, Jan used hula hoops placed in a chalk tray to create a Venn diagram. Students received sticky notes to place in the correct parts of the hoops to create the diagram. Then students wrote in journals what the Venn diagram told them. This hands-on problem-solving and writing experience used the strengths of both male and female brains.

➡ *Simple Machines:* For third-grade students who needed extra help with conceptualization in a unit on simple machines, Jan brought in simple machines (a lever, fulcrum, load, and so forth) for the students to manipulate. They had to figure out how to move the load, what made it easier or harder, and so on. A group of three boys figured it out very quickly. A group of three girls struggled and did not figure it out until they were guided.

➡ *Pie Notes:* Rita Oglesby discovered a way to teach the value of notes in music. She used the appropriate segments of a pie to indicate the notes (one-quarter of the pie equals quarter notes, half of the pie equals half notes). The results were striking—especially with boys who had been bored and somewhat difficult. The boys liked the physical activity involved, showed pride in their accomplishments, and generated a competitive spirit in solving problems with the manipulatives.

➡ *TERC Series:* Columbia, Missouri, schools use "Investigations in Number, Data, and Space," the K–5 mathematics curriculum developed by

TERC, which offers students meaningful mathematical problems and emphasizes depth in mathematical thinking. TERC is a nonprofit educational research and development organization; its mission is to improve mathematics, science, and technology teaching and learning. It creates curricula and other products and develops applications of new technologies.

Mixing Modalities and Strategies

Girls enjoy variety in teaching. Often, when a student is having a problem with a subject, he or she becomes bored or feigns boredom. This is one way the learning brain defends when it feels that it is inadequate. Variety in learning modality stimulates the brain past the defensive mask so that learning can occur.

➡ *Writing:* Writing tasks can be incorporated into the teaching of all subjects. When combined with spatial or manipulative learning, they provide a way for girls to express their understanding. For example, match math and science lessons with journal writing so that girls can use their writing strengths to help them process math calculations and science data.

➡ *Acting/Role Playing:* Some forms of acting and role playing can be used in teaching math and science (for example, mixing "apples" and "oranges," representing fractions). The movement involved appeals to boys' brains, and the relationships appeal to girls'.

➡ *Concrete Tactile Experiences:* Montessori classrooms use number rolls, number chains, and other manipulatives to teach math and science. Such experiences help students who lack abstract or spatial perception.

➡ *Peer Tutoring and Teaching:* Many students benefit from peer tutoring and teaching. When Denise Young sees girls doing group work in an area they don't feel as comfortable in, she adds a boy or two to their group. In a science unit on simple machines, the girls really got into the activities when the boys encouraged them.

➡ *Group Work:* Working in teams and groups helps students learn math and science. Denise did an estimation unit and used jars of items to predict accuracy. Using the jars and working in groups, boys and girls had better results.

Montessori classrooms also use group learning and partnered learning.

➡ *Role Modeling:* Denise adds role models to the mix of learning experiences, especially for girls. She talks about her Tae-Bo kick boxing class and she picks girls for activities or jobs that boys usually do, such as carrying boxes.

In terms of the brains and learning needs of girls, role modeling and encouragement often outweigh specific academic issues. Girls appear to have a weakness in the area of risk taking. Encouraging a girl toward risk taking in learning enriches the individual girl and the classroom. Teachers say that many girls' brains can do almost anything if their wills and spirits are encouraged.

Use of Computers and Other Media

There are many uses for the computer in the classroom. Boys often learn better with the fast action and excitement of games than with lessons. Girls can increase spatial connections (and later business and workplace competence) through early computer use. However, it is essential to be cautious about computer use for children under nine. Brain research shows that, as with everything else we put into a child's brain, computer and media stimulants are potentially harmful.

Jane Healy's *Failure to Connect* is a crucial reference, as is *Screen Smarts,* by Gloria De Gaetano and Kathleen Bander. Here are some research findings:

- Attention-span problems may be the result of early brain attachment to mechanical stimulation that does the brain's work for it and does not compel areas of the brain (such as the temporal lobe and left hemisphere) to grow normally. This is a special problem for boys because their brains do not naturally grow as quickly in these areas. The young male's brain (right hemisphere) is attracted to spatial stimulants, such as moving objects on computer screens; these stimulants ensure that his left hemisphere does not grow as well.
- Imagination functions of the brain, especially in the right hemisphere, do not grow as richly when young brains are attached to mechanical stimulants.

- Reading, writing, and verbal skills develop more slowly if young brains are mechanized too early. Reading and writing are whole-brain activities that require the use of many brain functions at once. Spatial stimulants (television, movies, and computer screens—especially when images move fast) reduce the time the young brain spends on whole-brain activity and increase its time on partial-brain activity. Thus, the whole brain does not develop as well and, because most such stimulants are less verbal than spatial, it is left-hemisphere development that is generally lost.

- It is crucial that schools and parents collaborate to discover how long a young child is using a computer, watching TV, or playing video games in a day. Often, a second- or third-grader's brain is getting more than enough screen time at home and does not need more than a few hours of computer time per week at school. By about fourth grade, the brain's imaginative, verbal, and attention functions are better developed, and computer time can increase.

- There is value in computer and technology programming, but not for younger children. A child who learns to use a computer at six and a child who learns at sixteen show little or no difference in proficiency after a few months of use, with no risk to natural brain development. The computer is a tool to be used in moderation, not to invade group dynamics, development of fine and gross motor skills, verbal and social development, and natural learning curves.

Middle School

According to the U.S. Department of Education, girls have nearly caught up to boys in math and science scores and now take more math and science than boys do. But at the top end of the scales (highest math and physics), boys still dominate. Given the configuration of the male brain—more focus on the right hemisphere, greater tendency toward high abstraction and design—males probably always will have a statistical advantage in higher math and science. However, within fifteen years, we have helped many girls find parity—a testament to what a schools can do to solve a brain-based and gender-based disparity.

Of course, many boys also have problems with math and science. So many of the innovations directed at brain-based math-and-science learning problems for girls are also helpful to boys.

Techniques to Encourage Learning

➡ *Cooperative Learning:* During mathematics, Lilly Figueroa finds that grouping students for activities takes the pressure off individual students. They are more confident and willing to volunteer answers (without looking "dumb") because they are group answers. The students learn to depend on one another's strengths.

➡ *Cooperative Learning Groups and Pairs:* Sheryl Sullivan forms cooperative groups so that girls will feel comfortable being participants and leaders. In the sixth grade, many girls become very self-conscious about themselves with boys, so she puts girls who lack confidence in math into groups with other girls. Sheryl puts girls who have strong math skills with boys who will allow them full participation and/or leadership. As their confidence builds, the group they are in becomes less of a concern.

➡ *Call-On Ratios:* When leading a discussion, it is important to find some parity in how many times one calls on shyer students, many of whom—in middle school math and science classes—are girls.

➡ *Showcasing Girls:* Anthony Becker tries to point out girls' talents in math and encourage them to pursue it. He also tries to call on girls an appropriate number of times to answer questions. He "showcases" them by asking them to take leadership positions, in order to help make them comfortable in their mathematical achievement.

➡ *Using a Variety of Approaches, Including Visual Aids:* Given how quickly the brain is growing during these years, variety is useful for engaging students' brains. When a child has a disadvantage, as some girls do in math, variety is even more important. Combining clear, complete, repeated instructions with overhead visuals and hands-on work visuals is multisensory and engages more of the brain in learning. Tanya Wittleson says,

"Visuals, like overheads, capture their attention. It is more like watching TV for them."

A program called *Hands-On Equations,*® by Henry Borenson, published by Phi Delta Kappa, provides a visual and kinesthetic introduction to algebraic concepts by removing the abstractness from algebra and making the concepts concrete. Teacher materials include manuals for Levels I, II, and III; worksheets; an answer key; and one student kit of game pieces with a flat, laminated balance for the teacher, two-dimensional balances for the students, pawns, and number cubes. There's also a demonstration video.

Ray McGowan offers other approaches to teaching girls math and science:

- When needed, separate girls from boys
- Pick field trips to places where females are in a position of dealing with math or science, thus providing role models
- Give directions over and over
- Emphasize hands-on work

Boys and Girls Need Some of the Same Things

Patricia Campbell, an educational consultant, studied key classroom characteristics that helped boys and girls in math and science. She discovered that effective classrooms:

- Allow no disrespect, whether teacher put downs of students or students of one another
- Use more than one instructional method, such as lecture, small groups, diagrams, and peer tutors (students learn best when they have variety)
- Do not allow a small group of attention seekers to dominate

Computer Science and Gender in Middle School and High School

There is a marked disparity between girls and boys in some essential computer-technology education, especially development of skills that translate into workplace success. According to a study by the AAUW, only 17 percent of high school students who take the advance placement tests in computer science are girls. Women earn only 28 percent of the bachelor's degrees in computer science and constitute just 20 percent of information-technology professionals. Some of this disparity is natural; girls may never want to design very abstract computer programs as much as boys. Even so, the disparity is frightening in an era in which fluency in the language and use of computers is crucial.

We can begin dealing with this disparity in middle school. As much as possible, teachers need to help girls deal with computer phobia; make sure that boys don't dominate computer use; and make sure that girls have the opportunity to learn computer languages as concretely as possible.

Some research shows that girls are at a disadvantage in acquiring technological skills. Despite male-female parity in Internet activity at home, parity in the classroom can be trickier to accomplish. Many males aggressively seek computer use, and most females step aside to allow the aggressive users to dominate computer time, especially where it is not possible to have one computer per student.

Many females do not gravitate toward the spatial stimulant of the computer screen as naturally as males do, and the female brain is not naturally inclined toward the kind of quick, right-hemisphere stimulation that computer games (especially fast-moving ones) generate. Girls don't play these games as frequently as boys and are more inclined to choose a verbalizing or relationship activity. The exceptions are chat-room use and Internet buying: surveys show that girls and boys pursue these two for about the same amount of time, although they buy different products, and girls are slightly more likely to stay longer in a single chat room, while boys are more likely to roam.

Girls need to learn computer technologies; our culture suffers for leaving them behind and may rob them of a chance to succeed. Furthermore, some girls do not attempt the most sophisticated computer programming technologies, as the spatial and abstract-computation elements of their brains are not as naturally developed as many males'. These girls must be encouraged to use computers in general and also to seek tutorial help for sophisticated uses. Teacher vigilance in this area is important. Girls need to have equal computer access time and female role models (from within the school and from the community) who know computers well and can build girls' interest in computer technology.

When teaching high-school computer science, Janet Rodgers noted the low numbers of girls in her classes and actively recruited female students. She learned that girls responded more to things such as definite problem solving; they shied away from the lone-wolf/hacker/gaming approach to computers held by many boys. As part of her doctoral coursework, she also found that girls who had very active support and encouragement from their fathers were able to navigate the traditional computer culture much more effectively.

Janet offers the following teaching techniques:

➡ *Gender-Specific Group Discussions:* At times, Janet met separately with groups of girls or boys from her computer programming classes to discuss issues. She found that students were more candid about classroom dynamics and concerns when talking in same-sex groups. Often, they conducted sexist tirades (for example, "Boys just want to play dumb computer games by themselves" and "I don't want any girl to be smarter than me; I'm glad we don't have many in class"). The most vociferous outpouring often was from the male who was the class-appointed computer guru.

These gender-specific discussions gave Janet information about how the class was really operating from the students' perspectives. She had not seen any signs of such strong sexist bias and hostility in class. She then began to look for subtle behaviors that reinforced "turf protecting," "girl shunning," and "dumb boy computer usage." She also found that girls, as well as many sensitive boys, became more active participants when gender-specific issues were confronted directly.

➡ *Real-Life Computer Programming Applications:* Janet sought areas in the school context that could use some customized computer software. Her classes worked on a grade-point-averaging program for the high school's teachers and on simple skill/drill math programs suitable for use by elementary school students. Her students developed the software, field tested numerous versions, and trained prospective users. This gave students the opportunity to provide valuable mentoring for the younger students and to present themselves as expert advisors to other adults in the high school setting.

➡ *A Cooperative, Team Approach for Projects:* Noting that girls become more active learners in group settings, Janet modeled cooperative, "team" approaches to many projects. Working with a team is essential for software development. Many boys in Janet's classes were truly gifted computer programmers but lacked the social skills necessary for working successfully with others, while girls who lacked superior technical savvy were often excellent communicators. Janet formed work groups, making sure that each group member was responsible for some aspect of the project. Still and animated graphics often were incorporated into the computer programs. More visual learners often conceptualized an animated effect that challenged the group.

➡ *Displaying the Work of Student Programmers:* Janet used public venues, such as the cafeteria and open-house gatherings, to showcase student work. A few computer screens were set up with rolling examples of student work (for example, animated greeting cards and quiz-show-format programs). These presentations encouraged students, especially girls, to sign up for more computer classes.

High School

The U.S. Commission on National Security and the National Commission on the Teaching of Mathematics and Science have stressed the need for more college graduates in science and computer science and for more science and math teachers, in order to properly manage science and technology in the coming decades.

Similarly, the National Conference on the Revolution in Earth and Space Science Education has called for reforms in education in this field—which integrates physics, biology, chemistry, geology, oceanography, meteorology, and all the life sciences. "Blueprint for Change," the conference report, cited the impact of this field on numerous aspects of life, including weather forecasts; crop production; urban planning; community development; management of energy, water, and other resources; social and economic policy making; and emergency preparedness.

The sciences also impact things as important as national security and the continuing existence of species on this planet. For the first time in history, students need to be familiar with basic math and some science in order to qualify for all but the most menial of jobs. And increasing numbers of math and science graduates and educators are needed.

Just as males often are at a disadvantage in school because they are in female-brain classrooms, many high school girls find themselves at a disadvantage in classrooms in which male math and science teachers teach to fit male brain systems. Nonspatial boys also can have difficulty with this.

The changes made in helping girls reach parity in math is inspiring. Girls now take as much math and science in high school as boys and test nearly at par (with the male brain advantage still evident at the highest, most abstract math and in physics). But some of the parity is because more girls finish school than boys.

Girls have difficulty learning some math, perhaps because they are not called on as much but also for biological reasons. Adolescent males receive surges of the hormone testosterone five to seven times a day; this can increase spatial skills, such as higher math. Increased estrogen during the menstrual cycle increases female performance in all skills, including spatials, so an adolescent girl may perform well on any test, including math, a few days per month. Males have a proclivity toward high abstraction, so they are better able to master abstract math than females and to enjoy it on a two-dimensional board. Girls often cannot master physics or calculus in high school, with everything written on the board and the boys and the teacher going so fast. Boys often make fun of them, injuring their self-esteem and making it even harder to learn.

We cannot affect hormonal dynamics, but we can innovate in math based on knowledge of the female brain. Some teachers are increasing the auditory aspect of a math lesson—putting it on the blackboard and on paper but also talking about it with the students. Adding verbalization to visual blackboard teaching helps girls and verbal boys to work through the lesson.

Techniques to Encourage Learning

➡ *Teach to Three Senses:* The more tactile and concrete a math or science lesson is, the easier it is for the widest variety of students. Visual (seeing), auditory (hearing), and tactile (touching, feeling) input engages three different senses.

➡ *Innovations to Help Girls:* Pay special attention to innovations that make high-level math accessible to girls, such as manipulatives, field trips, journaling, and note taking.

➡ *Building a Tepee:* A friend from the Blackfoot tribe taught Jeri Buckley how to erect a tepee. By presenting the technique in class as an engineering challenge, she helped students realize that the Blackfoot people's solution was scientific. As it was traditionally women's work, the question was "How could two Blackfoot women erect a tepee three times as tall as they were without using a ladder?" As small groups worked on their models with dowels, string, and rectangles of cloth, they soon realized that they needed to tie the dowels together near the tops to get them to balance against one another when they were upright. A greater challenge was how to get the poles upright. The students also had to imagine how the women could wrap the full-size tepee cover in place, two to three feet above them. This science lesson included small-group brainstorming, trial-and-error learning, group problem solving, and a multisensory experience. It created group bonds early in the school year. The cultural history added depth and interest.

Even if all students are learning well, this type of whole-brain experience should be done for its own sake, many times during the year. As the adolescent brain increases its abstract abilities, it seeks these integrative experiences.

Through such activities, the abstracting mind makes larger intuitive leaps than it can make in a "read the problem, write the solution" exercise.

➡ *Reinforce Lessons with Various Techniques:* Chris Christopher, who teaches trigonometry and strategies (senior math), gives homework related to a lesson presented that day, as many students do not really learn the concepts until after the class goes over the homework the next day. Chris also uses various techniques to reinforce the concepts (for example, games, review, group work, students doing problems in front of the class, and extra help). For example, he teaches a lesson, then has students discuss something different or play a game, then returns to the lesson to see what they remember. He tries to do something out of the norm to help students remember. He finds that the success of activities depends on the grade level and personalities of the students as well as the time of day, which affects their energy levels and what types of activities they feel like doing.

➡ *Who Wants To Be a Math Whiz? and Other Games:* Chris uses games based on the formats of Twenty Questions, Bingo, "Jeopardy," "The Match Game," and "Who Wants To Be a Millionaire?" Most of the questions are related to what is being taught in the classroom. The prizes may be stickers, candy, or small objects of interest. Some math puzzles and logic games can be played at any time of the year and involve students in the subject from different approaches.

➡ *Solving As You Go:* In his strategies (senior math) class, Chris solves math problems as he teaches, at the same time as his students, so that he is not leading them to answers and they are more likely to actually understand rather than simply pretend to understand. As they find the solutions together, Chris helps the students to be proud of their input.

➡ *Varying One's Voice and Presentation:* Chris tries to avoid speaking in a monotone and varies his presentation with different voices and sound effects. If he suspects that students are not paying attention, he switches to a very low voice so that they have to strain to hear. He also uses body language to help keep the students interested.

Language, Reading, Writing, and Social Science

ONE OF THE FINEST RESOURCES A TEACHER CAN CONSULT TO IMPROVE TEACHING OF language arts and literacy is *Teaching Children to Be Literate,* by Manzo and Manzo. The Manzos are brain-based researchers and are trained in other areas of literacy learning.

Preschool and Kindergarten

Boys generally need more help than girls in developing language skills. Self-directed activities, using the real world, and other strategies useful for spatial development also enhance language development.

Using Movement, Manipulatives, and Props

The following demonstrate the opportunities boys have to grow when they are allowed to be mentally, physically, and socially active:

➡ *Showcase Books:* Have books on shelves and elsewhere around the classroom so that boys who don't feel comfortable with reading can get used to the presence of books.

➡ *New Shoes:* Kathi Winkler uses songs with finger plays daily to encourage language development. Boys participate most readily with and request songs in which their whole bodies are involved. With a song called "Late Last Night," someone puts different shoes on your feet while you "sleep." The music then encourages things like riding a motorcycle wearing boots and running to score a touchdown wearing cleats. The anticipation of running or jumping encourages boys to sing the song and helps to increase vocabulary.

➡ *Holding Props:* Laurie, a speech and language specialist, tells stories to the children while each holds a prop central to the tale. A child with articulation errors at times is reluctant to talk but, with a prop in his hand, he is more attentive and his spontaneous language increases.

➡ *Feeling Board:* Have a permanent "feeling cork board" on which balloons are taped above the words "angry," "sad," "happy," and "mad"; let the kids throw safe, plastic darts at the feelings they are having, which gives them an action for accessing and then talking about the feelings.

➡ *Whole-Brain Activities:* A young boy had a moderate language delay and did not want to be read to or learn to write. After twelve months of preschool, he set up ramps on classroom shelves and rolled cars down them. As the cars took flight and landed several feet away, two other boys became interested. As the boy worked to keep control of his activity (spatial task), his brain developed good patterning and he spoke in clear, complete sentences of five to eight words—on target for his age.

As the cars flew off the ramps, they often were lost under shelves and coat racks. The three boys worked together to find a solution. One found a plastic bowl and put it on the floor below the ramps. The boys engaged in discussion and argument to find a satisfactory adjustment to the ramp and bowl. When they realized that cars sometimes went different distances, they added two more bowls and a basket. As the role of leader was vied for, verbal negotiation skills were tried out. Kathi intervened once to say that the boys had to figure out how to take turns, and they resolved this verbally.

Kathi inserted some writing and math skills into the activity. Since boys tend to be competitive, she suggested that they keep score of how many times their cars hit the targets. The boys made efforts at writing their names, and she showed them how to keep score.

This illustrates how right-brain spatial work and left-brain language work come together through a whole-brain activity (requiring spatials, verbal language, social interaction, and emotional self-management).

A similar activity works for girls; the challenge is to create one that girls like. This may involve a verbally interactive game, such as "Hospital," in which the girl is asked to use pencil and paper to record how many patients come in and what their symptoms are.

Elementary School

Reading and writing are basic to academic and social success. For neurological reasons, many boys are further behind in these skills, but many girls also have difficulties.

Our research grouped all subjects not in the math and science area as "language arts." The following innovations have worked for teachers of these classes.

Techniques to Encourage Learning

➡ *Reading to Stuffed Animals:* Stacy Moyer teaches first grade children who are learning English as a second language. She finds that the children enjoy reading to the stuffed animals she puts in the book corner. Shy students often feel more comfortable talking to the animals at first. Later, they often take turns reading to one another and the animals.

➡ *Providing Things to Write About:* Stacy says that when she lets students write about the topics of their choice, she gets more out of them. She provides interesting objects and experiences in the classroom (such as caterpillars turning into chrysalides and then butterflies and plants growing from seeds) and the children often choose to write about these things.

➡ *Using Graphic Organizers:* Stacy finds that using graphic organizers (ways of helping students to organize information) helps second-language

learners to write longer passages and to use more varied vocabulary. Stacy uses simple Venn diagrams and word webs. Using a word web, for example, if the class is writing about ducks, Stacy would write "ducks" in the center of the paper and circle it. The students would brainstorm what they know about ducks. Stacy would draw lines out from the word "ducks" to words the students generate (for example, "food," "ducklings," "habitat") and then draw lines from those areas (for example, "habitat" might have lines to "ponds," "lakes," and "nests"; "ducklings" might have lines to "fuzzy," "little," "hatch," and "eggs"). Stacy often draws pictures beside the words on word webs and other organizers to help her students remember what the words mean.

Useful Websites for more information on these techniques are: The Graphic Organizer (www.graphic.org), S.C.O.R.E. (www.score.k12.ca.us), and the Innovative Learning Group (www.thinkingmaps.com).

➡ *Journaling:* Jan has her students write something that they did or did not like about each day in their journals. (See "Yays and Yucks" in Chapter Two, "Bonding and Attachment.") The students with poor writing skills find it difficult, but it gives them a good ritual and good practice.

Angie Hathaway puts a journal question on the blackboard that is academically related or something the kids do outside class. She sets up discussions and debates of issues related to their needs or interests (for example, "Would you rather have recess or physical education?").

➡ *Waiting for an Answer:* Denise Young noticed that some students, especially boys with less-developed verbal skills, need extra time to formulate thoughts. She uses the sixty-second wait time with boys when asking a question and she gets better responses from them. This technique is also useful with girls who are not quick to answer when asked a question about a story or process.

➡ *Extra Encouragement for Girls:* Ruth makes sure she calls on each girl each day. Girls tend not to believe in themselves until they receive encouragement, and they need more positive feedback than they typically receive. Rather than risk failure, girls tend to stand back if they don't think they can do something. It is crucial that teachers realize how personally girls can take perceived failure—in a relationship or in academic performance.

Patricia Henley says that teachers can help girls find the ability and perseverance to be winners. One girl thought she couldn't speak publicly. Patricia gave her repeated opportunities to speak to her and to groups of students or teachers. Finally, the girl was selected to be a peer mediator. She couldn't have done it without encouragement and praise each step of the way.

➡ *Female Role Models and Nonbiased Materials:* The importance to girls of paired conversation, one-on-one encouragement, and role models cannot be overstated. Tell stories and use images of girls and women who are competent and who model varieties of mature female behavior.

Lois J. Hedge uses literature and materials that are not gender-biased in her classroom. She tries to be a role model for all students, especially for girls. Allowing girls to see females in many positive roles is a way to instill a sense of worth. Girls like to work together and help others. She helps to steer them to things that might empower them.

Jennifer Hull models behavior, dress, and courage in an attempt to show girls how to be strong, intelligent, and feminine.

Using Manipulatives

Give boys, especially, lots of things to touch and otherwise sense, especially when reading and writing are being taught.

➡ *Making Words Tactile:* Stacy uses tactile activities to work on sight words (words such as "the," "you," and "have," which appear often in reading texts and which students should know "on sight" and be able to read quickly). Students make a word out of dough, write it in shaving cream, or glue tissue paper to a big written version of the word.

➡ *Magnetic Letters:* Monica Miller uses "hands-on" learning as much as possible. When a student is learning a new word, she has the child move magnetic letters to create the new word, read the word aloud, move the magnetic letters to reform the word, reread the word, and repeat the process. Repetition is good for reinforcing new skills in the young child.

➡ *Alphabet Blocks:* Monica finds that alphabet blocks are helpful for the boys in developing letter recognition as well as in developing fine motor skills.

➡ *Read and Draw:* A second-grade teacher's students love to be read to. She allows them to draw as she reads, and many of them are especially attentive and creative in this modality. Seeing what students draw gives insight into their lives. Boys tend to draw robots, violent scenes, and military or sports themes. Girls tend to draw flowers, natural scenes, and realistic situations. Drawing is not a substitute for reading, but it can take the pressure off those children who read poorly but use aural and verbal stimulation better to code and decode words.

➡ *New-Word Letter Packets:* Jan Miller created letter packets for each child, to teach new vocabulary words in a story. Kids seemed excited about finding the words in the story. Each child was given a bright index card to follow along in the book while the story was read. This seemed to keep students on track with the story.

➡ *Stress Balls:* Jan allows each student to handle a stress ball while reading a story or while she is reading a story aloud. Many of the boys perform better if they have something to do with their hands.

➡ *Macaroni:* To make writing fun, Jan uses macaroni in several shapes to represent apostrophes, quotation marks, and commas. Boys respond to having concrete objects to work with.

Providing Various Learning Modalities

Many boys find one learning mode they like and stick with it, whereas girls generally like moving from one mode to another—probably a reflection of the multitasking female brain. Although some boys also enjoy a variety of learning modes, girls usually shine when provided with numerous ways of learning.

➡ *Seeing, Feeling, and Hearing New Words:* When her students are learning a new letter or word, Stacy Moyer has them "write" the letter or word on one another's backs. They say the letters as they write and then say the word (for example, "t . . . h . . . e . . . the"). As they do this, she holds a large card that has the word on it, so they can see it, feel it, and hear it.

Stacy's students clap as they spell new words orally. She adds a motion at the end; for example, when learning the word "out," they clap and say "o . . . u . . . t," then they shout "out" and use a thumb motion like an umpire's "out." When learning the word jump, they say "j . . . u . . . m . . . p," shout "jump," and then jump.

➡ *Storytelling:* Offer lots of storytelling and myth creation in the classroom to help the male brain develop its imaginative and verbal skills.

➡ *Acting:* Many children, especially girls, enjoy acting out a poem, story, or play. They may simply assume characters and make appropriate gestures while the piece is being read aloud, or they may be given (or choose) roles and prepare a presentation of the piece. They often want to wear costumes and make and use props. This opens the way for learning about the lives, clothes, food, homes, implements, and so on, of historic and fictional characters.

Acting also allows shyer children to step outside themselves and explore a range of new behaviors that they might not exhibit otherwise.

➡ *Role Playing:* Role playing can be used in teaching most subjects. This provides movement that appeals to boys' brains and conversation that appeals to girls.' Assuming the roles and acting as the characters might also allow students to experiment with new behaviors and topics in a "safe" way.

➡ *Multisensory Stimulation:* Denise asked students to write Halloween stories. She played scary music and lit candles. She got great stories from the boys. They used a lot more "describing" words when listening to the music.

➡ *Tutoring Others:* A social-studies teacher says that her female students enjoy tutoring other students, male or female, the same age or younger.

➡ *Cooperative Groups:* She also finds that cooperative groups help the girls be more creative and confident. It also can be helpful to pair poorer readers with better readers for research projects and reports.

Jennifer Hull also creates small groups. The girls especially enjoy grouping around her desk and talking about how literature affects them.

➡ *Separate-Sex Learning:* Powerful research has revealed the benefits of separate-sex learning for girls. Ruth Whertvine's school separated the girls from the boys and finds that it helps the girls to concentrate. They are more focused.

➡ *Read Across America Day:* Friday, March 1, is "Read Across America Day," sponsored by the National Education Association to commemorate the birthday of Dr. Seuss (Ted Geisel). On this day each year, schools across the United States highlight reading, with parents, celebrities, members of the armed forces, and other volunteers coming into the schools to read to children and donate books. At some schools, students and teachers dress as Dr. Seuss characters.

Middle School

According to the Department of Education, boys are about a year and a half behind girls in reading and writing skills. Some disparity favoring girls probably will always exist, owing to the female's left-hemisphere focus and development, but within ten to fifteen years, if we do for reading and writing what we've done for math and science, we should bring the disparity down significantly.

Techniques to Encourage Learning

➡ *Scholarly Discourse:* Carol Jago trains her students in "the rules of scholarly discourse," which she learned from Yvonne Hutchinson. The rules of scholarly discourse are that

1. Students must talk to one another, not just to the teacher or the air.
2. Students must listen to one another. They must either address the previous speaker or offer a reason for changing the subject.
3. Students must be prepared to participate. (If not prepared to respond, the appropriate response is, "I'm not sure what I think about that; please come back to me.")

➡ *The Seminar Method:* Carol also teaches another innovation, the "seminar," which is run by her students without her involvement until the end. The rules are as follows:

1. Everyone must participate at least once during the seminar.
2. No student needs to raise a hand to be called on, but all have to look around and take notice of shy classmates (for example, "Luke, you look as though you disagree. What are you thinking?").
3. Students learn how to manage compulsive talkers (for example, "Just when the motor mouth inhales, insert a comment").
4. Silence is allowed, especially while someone is thinking. This is a time for students to open the book and find a passage to ponder, rather than jump into another person's thinking pause.

Carol doesn't correct students' content during their discussions, but she might comment on their conduct. Her job is mainly to teach them the skills of scholarly discussion. Carol talks about her methods in *With Rigor for All: Teaching the Classics to Contemporary Students.* Her methods lead to mature, inclusive discussions that rein in but do not punish the attention seekers (many of whom are males), make the class responsible for helping shy members (usually girls), and teach history and literature to minds starved for stories from elders. The seminar method can be used to teach almost any subject.

→ *Connecting Language Arts to Other Experiential Processes:* Sharon Fisher connects language arts to her girls' rite-of-passage group. This gives the girls a deep connection with some of the material they are reading.

Darla Novick finds interesting subject matter in unusual places: A judge let her know of items coming up in court that would be good for the kids (especially the boys) to observe. Her class visited court often, and many class assignments grew from these visits.

→ *Movement:* It is essential to increase physical movement during the school day. Movement helps release pent-up energy; cut down on discipline problems; and stimulate the bored, tuning-out brain. Brandy Barnett plans lessons that involve getting up to do things. It has invigorated her class learning.

→ *Graphic Organizers:* Using graphic organizers (diagrams that show relationships between words and topics) can help boys—as well as many girls—in taking notes, understanding relationships, and organizing content for writing projects. (See the references to useful Websites under "Elementary School.") Typical graphic organizers are

- Cause-and-effect diagrams and fishbone diagrams

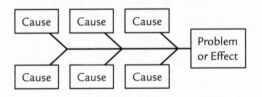

- Continuums

High |____|____|____|____| Low

- Cycles

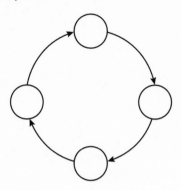

- Flow charts

- Grids, matrix diagrams, and tables

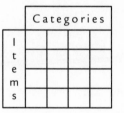

- Hierarchies and tree diagrams

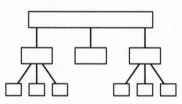

- Similes (compare two things by using "like" or "as")

  "Jeffrey is as busy as a bee."

- Metaphors (apply words or phrases to objects they don't usually denote)

  "His father was a tower of strength."

- Mind maps and word (spider) webs

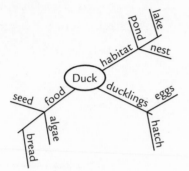

- Venn diagrams

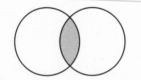

➡ *Note-Taking Innovations:* Girls and boys can have difficulty with note taking. Girls may become preoccupied taking down everything a teacher or another student says. Boys may not keep up with quick discussions or instructions, and their note taking is often shoddy.

Brenda Bock's teaching team trains incoming sixth graders in how to take notes. In all subject areas, they give out a full copy of the notes and go over them orally, step by step. Later, they make skeletal outlines with spaces for the students to fill in. Finally, the students take the notes themselves.

➡ *Buddy Note Taking:* Lilly Figueroa provides a notebook and carbon and assigns a student to take notes, making a copy for a student who is not a good note taker or one who is absent. This makes the note takers feel important and they tend to take better notes because they are doing it for someone else.

➡ *Multisensory Learning:* Brenda's team also strives for multisensory learning, using visual overheads and hard copy, auditory lectures and discussion, and the kinesthetic act of taking notes.

➡ *Topical Projects by Gender:* Girls often are bored reading the many books about males. In social studies and American history classes, Brian Zipfel has students pick historical topics from the unit being studied (often including women in history) and select ways to present their projects. This lets girls use their verbal and linguistic strengths. They often create dramatic presentations.

High School

Teaching Reading

The vast majority of reading-traumatized and reading-deficient high school students are males. As they become more defensive, angrier, and more isolated, many start skipping classes and may drop out of school. Teachers may be unable to reach them. The following are some suggestions for helping reading-deficient students:

➡ *Diminish Repetitive Auditory Stimulation for Some:* Some students (especially males) complain that teachers "talk too much." For nonverbal, nonauditory students, this may be "boring" (frustrating). Being read to over and over does not work for them, and they may be unable to process complex vocabulary and subtextual material as easily as their female (or more verbal) classmates. Some such students may be classified as LD when, in fact, they merely need and seek left-hemisphere stimulation.

➡ *Enhance Auditory Stimulation for Some.* A similar situation faces some students, who, instead of finding auditory presentation of complex word sequences difficult, actually need it to help them compensate for visual difficulties in decoding complex texts. These students can benefit from more group or partnered reading aloud.

➡ *Help in Analyzing Text:* Whether students need more or less auditory stimulation, they almost certainly require parsing of text into discrete units (syntactic functions) that can be analyzed separately.

➡ *Tactile, Manipulative Experiences:* Most students also benefit from having concrete manipulative experiences interspersed with reading experiences—tactile (physical) learning that integrates reading with other lessons.

Gail finds that her boys learn better if hands-on activities are part of a literary lesson that integrates the arts, geography, social studies, and math. In one lesson for students with reading difficulties, she assigned them research projects on continents (a continent's area and size, facts about the countries in it, and so forth). She let students draw the continents on large cardboard sheets, then paint them, then use papier mâché to build the mountains and waterways. The students had to research and make notebooks about their continents. This was very effective for poorer readers paired with better readers.

In another lesson, Gail was teaching parts of the *Iliad* and the *Odyssey*, which led to a research project on the Trojan War. She first set a reading assignment. Then students made Trojan horses. A particularly moody boy did some extra-credit research and meticulously built a model of the Greek Parthenon. Engaged by the physical task, he learned more about the assigned literature. His brain could attach scenes, words, and other content to objects to enhance literacy learning.

➡ *Using Media That Teens Enjoy:* In an English class at Randolph, Massachusetts, High School, students watched the "Simpsons" version of Shakespeare's *Macbeth;* they responded to it much better than they did to the black and white movie version.

Teaching Language

➡ *Language Rally:* In a Spanish class at Randolph High School, students were given index cards that had different directions on them in Spanish. The students had to follow the directions until they arrived at certain places.

➡ *Nonverbal Communication Activities:* Teenagers can be taught the benefits of understanding others' nonverbal communication, with applications to general communication as well as to cross-gender communication (psychosocial education). They also can be helped to realize what their nonverbal communication is saying to others. Older teens are able to understand nuance in tone of voice, pitch, and pacing as well as in physical gestures and other body language. This can be taught in a number of ways, including structured and unstructured role plays, "guessing" activities, and pantomimes.

A PROMISING LANGUAGE PROGRAM   Our research shows that reading and writing difficulties are a primary reason for male dysfunction in school. If a high school student has difficulty reading, his self-esteem plummets, core identity development is more difficult, and the future becomes frightening. Success in reading turns a young person back to the bonds, attachments, and other social supports that he needs to develop as a healthy person. In this sense, literacy in high school can be a secret to decoding adulthood.

Language!, developed by Jane Fell Greene, is a promising program for helping deficient high school–age readers. Teachers can be trained in it and use it right away. Its innovative, three-tiered approach fits what we know of adolescent brain development and areas of reading trouble denoted as male-brain deficiencies.

Based on the premise that high school learners need a literacy program that fits their phase of development, *Language!* teaches essential phonemics on three levels: basic literacy, testing the student along the way, and "literature learning."

At level one, the student learns phonemic awareness, decoding, encoding, fluency in passage reading, increased vocabulary, comprehension, and basic grammar. Writing and editing, even if rudimentary, are foundational. The student is tested until he reaches a level of mastery sufficient for progress. These essential developmental skills (for example, phonemic awareness) are not interrupted by expectations of mastery of higher-level skills (such as reading *To Kill a Mockingbird*). A student can try if he wishes, but it is accepted that he won't "get" a lot of it.

On level two, students are introduced to new strands, such as more sophisticated syllabication (polysyllabic words), greater vocabulary, morphology (Latin roots), and syntactically more complex sentences. Expository writing, appropriate for this level, is emphasized. The student is encouraged to read "higher-up" texts than he is able to fully decode at this level, but competence for this level does not include the expectation of level-three mastery.

In the level-three material, literature enters the picture. Metaphor, theme, point of view, plot development, and other elements of sophisticated literacy are now taught, along with Greek morphology. Over many months, sometimes years, these three levels build. At level three, the teacher can start testing the student on *To Kill a Mockingbird.*

This multitasking, brain-based, developmental program comes with computer software and other technologies. Like most successful achievement-support programs, the effectiveness of *Language!* stretches beyond academic success to increased self-confidence and personal development in other areas. One student's observation about the program was, "I always knew there must be some kind of secret to reading, but nobody had taught me the code."

Teaching Social Science

➡ *Making the Teacher and Subject More Interesting:* To get students interested in the history lesson plan at the beginning of the year, Paul Kaplan performs a rap previewing the year's subjects.

➡ *Propaganda:* Paul's students are asked to generate slogans to encourage events in history (for example, the French Revolution).

➡ *Using TV and Movies:* Paul runs episodes of "The Three Stooges" while students are studying the Great Depression, to illustrate how those movie shorts showed people living during the Depression that they could take a break from their troubles and laugh.

➡ *Invention Day:* Paul's students come up with any inventions they think are needed in the world; on Invention Day, a panel of judges and the other students rate the inventions in several different categories.

USING MOVEMENT AND MANIPULATIVES

➡ *Role Playing:* Paul's students re-enacted the meeting of the Three Estates before the French Revolution. Each student was assigned a role, and the activity was filmed.

➡ *Using Props:* Paul's class role played Archduke Francis Ferdinand's assassination using water guns. Another role play demonstrated what it was like to dodge bullets in WWII by having some students armed with silly string and water guns as another student carried a backpack loaded with weights and tried to escape.

LESSONS IN CHARACTER AND VALUES

➡ *Character Assessments:* Each student in Paul's class chooses another student in the class whom he or she has known for several years and lists the other's good and bad character traits. Afterward, the students reflect on the truth of the assessments and add their own comments. This is tied to a lesson on Napoleon, whose character the students also assess.

➡ *World Superstars:* Each of Paul's students is assigned a "world superstar," such as Jackie Robinson or Rosa Parks, and is required to give a report to the class as though he or she is that person. Then, to give the students some choice and opportunity to use their personal talents, each student can choose one "project" to complete the activity, such as a collage, song, or poem that reflects the superstar's contribution.

➡ *Report Card:* Paul's students make out a report card on a lesson subject, such as aspects of Great Britain's imperial rule over India.

➡ *Where Do You Stand?* To help students become more aware of their beliefs and values, Paul has students place themselves on the political spectrum and state their stances on domestic issues.

CONNECTING WITH THE COMMUNITY

➡ *Guest Speakers:* Paul Kaplan often has speakers who use history in their everyday lives come into the classroom; in his law and justice class, he had members of the Jury Commission come in to talk about jury duty.

➡ *Field Trips:* Paul takes students in his law and justice class to the Dedham House of Correction, where they speak with inmates, take a tour, and learn how things are run.

Field trips do not necessarily involve leaving the school building; students often just enjoy getting out of their seats for a while.

➡ *Visiting the Elderly:* Paul's students visit the elderly to speak with those who have actually experienced the events discussed in his history classroom. This makes the lesson more real and encourages a sense of community and interaction with the elderly.

6

Physical Learning and Nutrition

MORE THAN 25 PERCENT OF CHILDREN IN THE UNITED STATES ARE OVERWEIGHT, and the same number do not regularly participate in the vigorous activity that is necessary for full development. Children are eating nonessential fats and carbohydrates in junk food and spending less time in physical labor than previous generations. They need planned physical exercise. Because they spend more time inside closed rooms than their ancestors did, they also need more time outside.

The Need for Physical Activity

Young children, especially boys, need to move around as they learn. Before third grade, chairs and desks should be movable, not kept in a row or fixed to the floor, and as much space should be available in the classroom as possible.

Some schools have cut back on recess. In some, keeping children indoors during recess is a discipline tool. Many schools are also diminishing physical education. These are profound mistakes and hinder complete brain development.

The brain grows in relation to its connection with physical activity and natural environments. In order to grow, it needs the body to move about, in fine motor tasks such as bead work and in gross motor tasks such as running and playing. If the brain doesn't get physical movement ("cutting-loose time"), especially in early and middle childhood, it is more likely to impel that movement inappropriately.

Given the high male metabolism and energy levels, most boys need physical release in order to self-manage behavior more than girls do. Neurologically, boys can become almost desperate for recess.

Recess is also important as a physical and socializing time for girls, who need nonstructured time to develop friendships and challenge relationship systems. In regard to body-image issues (notably their fear of being overweight), which begin around third grade, it is essential that girls get exercise.

Especially until just before puberty, the brain develops sensory functions constantly. A seven-year-old might smell a rose in a way that an adolescent or adult does not. The child is building the cell patterns, tissues, and neurotransmissions throughout the brain that the adolescent and adult will rely on throughout life for patterning smells.

Play that goes on outside and in nature usually involves a complexity of social relations. That each child must manage the constant possibility of random experience is also good for the developing brain; it involves neural challenges regarding how hierarchies work and how the limbic system should accept or reject certain emotional impulses, from anger to joy. The outdoor environment also affords more space for physical movement, which, in turn, develops the brain. This is especially important for boys, because of their emphasis on the right hemisphere and their need for space in work and play.

Preschool and Kindergarten

Developing Fine Motor Skills

➡ *Sewing and Beadwork:* These help children learn fine motor skills (in which boys are weaker than girls).

➡ *Cutting and Tearing Paper:* Monica Miller's kindergarten classes do a lot of cutting and tearing of paper into smaller pieces (for creating collages) to increase fine motor skills.

The Outdoor Classroom

The outdoor classroom (a school's grounds, garden, and play area and other nature areas) is as important as the indoor, especially for younger children. It is a world of play, fantasy, and spiritual connection with nature—an essential component of the ultimate classroom.

➡ *Taking It Outdoors:* Young children are as much creatures of nature as culture, and nature is a great ally in teaching them. Especially in the early school years, sitting and being quiet is, to a great deal, about crowd control, not learning. Many children, especially boys, need to move around in order to learn. There is hardly a reading, writing, mathematical, or scientific lesson that cannot benefit from being taken to the natural world. This is especially useful for boys (and some girls) who seem to need to move all the time. Ages ago, boys had more space to move around in, so their impulsiveness was less an issue. Their brains still crave space to roam in. The more time they can spend outdoors, the more space for them to discover and navigate.

➡ *Nature Walks:* Monica Miller, who teaches a combination kindergarten-first grade class, finds that movement is very important to young learners. Her class goes on a lot of nature walks in the neighborhood (especially in the fall and spring) to observe the changes in the season, trees, leaves, flowers, birds, and animals. She has students who come to school not knowing colors or names of things such as treetops and branches. The walks help develop visual recognition (for example, a tree trunk is brown, and so are some of the leaves, the squirrels, and the picnic benches).

➡ *King of the Hill:* Eilene Green and her colleagues know that many boys misbehave as a way of striving for the attention and power, albeit negative, that uncontrolled impulsive behavior can bring. The more power a child feels, the less he misbehaves. Behind their school are stairs that rise toward a meadow. Children are encouraged to climb "above" the others. "Look how high you are; you're a king up there." The child giggles and feels very important.

➡ *Water Sounds:* One school built a playground on the roof, where water falling on rocks and a babbling brook soothe children's working brains. Bubbling fountains inside classrooms also can calm children and open their energy to greater learning.

➡ *Utilize Existing Organizations:* Outdoor and nature organizations are forming partnerships with schools and communities to teach children to appreciate and care for the natural world. For example, the National Wildlife Federation can help schools (even kindergartens) turn their grounds into nature-teaching areas.

Elementary School

Movement and Motor Skills

Meaningful Movement for Children presents a plan for integrating other elementary school curricula with physical education. Hoffman, Young, and Klesius present a set of learning themes around which it is possible to organize many of the learning activities in a school. These themes include awareness (including spatial awareness and manipulative abilities); independence (including following directions and making choices); communicating (including accepting and expressing feelings and ideas); accepting responsibilities and acting cooperatively; improving response; and relationships (including developing healthful patterns of living, understanding influences on the environment, and developing informed decision-making behavior). The themes reflect fundamental cognitive, affective, and motor tasks that all students must master, and the many suggested learning activities address all three aspects of a child's development.

➡ *Movement Songs and Games:* Monica Miller uses movement songs and games with young children. Traditional playground games are Duck, Duck, Goose; Red Light, Green Light; Mother May I?; and Lucy Locket. These help develop skills in listening and following directions. Monica says that some good tapes are by Raffe and Fred Prenner. They also teach children about colors, shapes, meanings of traffic signs and lights, weather, and so on. A tape called "Can a Cherry Pie Wave Good-Bye?" also includes playground games and movements.

➡ *Manipulatives in Learning Centers:* To help boys develop fine motor skills, Monica places manipulative activities in learning centers (for example, Play-Doh® and coloring-book pages in the art center to help develop coordination; cookie cutters, rolling pins, plastic utensils, and dishes to help manipulative skills in pouring, mixing, and setting a table).

Sports and Athletics

Although classrooms often can use a few games and other competitive exercises, we generally think of sports as too competitive for younger children. We recommend that a child not be placed in a competitive extracurricular sport until about the age of seven, unless the child specifically requests it. Competitive, organized sports (outside of mandatory physical education) are not crucial for healthy brain development before that age, so any competitive pressure in these sports is generally harmful. It imprints competitive use of the body at a time when, developmentally, children want to enjoy their use of their bodies without external pressure to perform.

After the age of seven, competitive sports can be added gradually to a child's curriculum. By fourth grade, many children actively seek competitive sports. However, not all children want to engage in team sports. Karate and tennis are good options for children in fourth grade and older. Regular physical activity—even running and jogging—is especially important for boys after about age ten, when the male body needs the activity to help it manage testosterone. Boys should be involved in some kind of rigorous, daily, physical activity of greater length than physical education class.

Organized sports for girls are also useful at these ages, not only to teach competition skills but also to help girls increase their muscle-to-fat ratios.

Some problems with sports stem from competitive coaches and parents, who push kids into competition too early. When athletics are cooperative as well as competitive, every participant receives some sort of prize. Parents are trained not to bark orders at kids, but to call out support.

The Outdoor Classroom

The suggestions under "Preschool and Kindergarten" above also apply to elementary schools.

➡ *Community Gardens:* Many communities have child-oriented gardens that can be visited on field trips. Often, these are connected to community centers, botanical gardens, and amusement venues. Children can engage their imaginations as they see, touch, smell, hear, and move through plants, rocks, and so on.

➡ *Growing Plants:* Children can grow plants from seed. This can be done indoors, on the classroom windowsill, or it can be done outdoors in a gardening area. Some schools have small gardens for each grade level, and the

children actually harvest flowers and vegetables. Children take great pride in watching the growth of even simple plants that they have nurtured.

➡ *Utilize Existing Organizations:* Teachers can find a wealth of information about teaching kids about nature from the National Wildlife Federation Website: www.nwf.org/kids/. Ranger Rick's Kids Zone contains games and suggestions for outdoor activities, as well as information about "Earthsavers," a club for elementary school students who want to learn more about nature and the environment.

The National Wildlife Federation also helps schools turn their grounds into wildlife habitats. For example, in the Orinda, California, school district, kindergarten through eighth-grade students grow threatened plants, study frog ponds, and work in organic vegetable gardens. Teachers use the areas to teach biology, math, and chemistry. The NWF has certified over 1,600 schools nationwide.

Middle School and High School

Sports and Athletics

We recommend mandatory sports or athletic activity for middle school students (between sixth and ninth grades). Like character education and school bonding systems, mandatory athletics can help cut down on discipline problems. Middle school is a time of enormous physical upheaval. Through directed physical activity, the brain learns to manage the body. For most boys, this is crucial in learning to self-manage testosterone. For girls, mandatory sports are useful in helping to develop skills that pertain to healthy physical competition. Studies show that both male and female students who have to develop self-discipline in sports are less likely to engage in drugs and other high-risk adolescent behavior. Students who don't like team sports can be directed to martial arts or other controlled physical activities that require self-discipline.

In high school, student choice can return, as tenth grade customarily is the time in which physical and hormonal upheavals ease. However, some extracurricular athletic activity ought to be mandatory. If sports become mandatory, schools must be vigilant in training coaches how to bond with and mentor, in healthy ways, the energy of youth. Coaches need to be trained in character education. In middle school especially, athletic success should be secondary to character education.

Mixed-Gender Sports

The needs of growing brains were not considered when schools moved toward mixed-gender sports activities, especially those that require high schoolers to engage in prolonged and intimate tactile contact. For the most part, gender innovations become counterintuitive when the social principle that "girls must do everything boys do and do it with boys" takes over cultural progress. Wrestling is a good example because it involves embarrassing tactile contact, which makes full accomplishment of the sport between males and females needlessly difficult. Jim Giunta, a former wrestling official, describes moves that require grabbing the lower midsection as difficult for males and females to do with each other. One coach has seen boys wrestling against girls become "wrecks" before their matches: "People don't understand when they talk about high school kids that they're children. They still have fragile egos." If a boy beats a girl, what is that worth to him? If she beats him, how will he face his friends?

Giving girls the opportunity to enjoy wrestling and to develop themselves through it is admirable but, like so many other areas of cultural innovation, wrestling is creating more strife than health for young people. Furthermore, adolescent embarrassment about girl-boy contact is developmentally appropriate and useful in reducing premature sexual behavior; it is not something we want to systematically decrease by trying to force this contact on high school boys and girls.

To ensure gender equity for girls in areas such as athletics, a school can promote physical and psychosocial safety by separating girls and boys in high-contact sports such as wrestling, football, and basketball. Gender tension in the school is lessened, and individual emotional stress is diminished. Ultimately, the school environment is more successful at its primary goal: protecting and encouraging developmentally appropriate human learning.

The Outdoor Classroom

➡ *Writing and Drawing in Nature:* At the Crestridge Ecological Reserve, in San Diego County, California, teenagers are asked to sit by themselves and write or draw. Formed by a partnership between schools and ecological organizations, the reserve also features talks by Kumeyaay peoples, whose ancestors lived in the mountainous region.

➡ *Utilize Existing Organizations:* The National Wildlife Federation Website: www.nwf.org/kids/ includes games and suggestions for outdoor activities, as well as information about "Teen Adventure," an NWF club for middle school students who want to learn more about nature and the environment.

For high school students, the site includes information about outdoor activities, as well as a link to "Earth Tomorrow," an NWF club for older teenagers.

Nutrition and Learning

Children need to eat the right foods at the right time. What they eat profoundly affects their ability to learn and behave. This is especially true of young children, who have not yet developed the ability to control their impulses or learn when under stress, including nutritional stress.

Parents need to be educated about nutrition; they often need help sifting through all the trends and messages in the media. Nutrition is a fundamental element of parent education coordination and school-home liaison. *The Biology of Success,* by Robert Arnot, explores the link between food and the brain.

➡ *Giving the Brain the Water It Needs:* From reading *Teaching with the Brain in Mind* (Jensen, 1998), Stacy Moyer is aware of the importance of the brain staying hydrated. She encourages her students to drink water, even though it means more trips to the restrooms.

Obesity

Childhood obesity has become a serious medical problem. Thirteen percent to one-fourth of all school-age children are overweight or obese—twice the numbers of twenty years ago. In May of 2002, the Centers for Disease Control and

Prevention reported that overweight children are being hospitalized at dramatically rising rates for diabetes, sleep apnea, asthma, gallbladder disease, and other conditions that obesity causes or worsens. There also is an increase of obesity-related diabetes, hypertension, and high blood pressure in Hispanic and black children.

Causes include home habits, day care, advertising, computer games, watching television, eating while watching television, fast foods, sugary soft drinks, restaurants, vending machines, malls, movie theaters, lack of safe playgrounds, and decline in physical play and other physical activity in schools (for example, recess and athletic programs) and in out-of-school time.

Carbohydrates, Proteins, and the School Day

The morning is not a good time for children to eat carbohydrates, especially if they need to settle into comfortable learning. High carbohydrates—such as toast, bagels, rolls, donuts, pasta, cereal (especially cereal with sugar), and other sugary foods—dull children's ability to learn. They are okay if a child is going to exercise first thing in the morning, as they generate quick energy (they bring blood sugar up from the low experienced during sleep). However, since children usually sit on the way to school and then sit in a classroom, a high-carbohydrate breakfast is not advisable.

Fast-release carbohydrates with a high glycemic index (refined sugars and refined grains, such as white bread) tell the brain to load the body up with glucose. They build up serotonin quickly, which can give a temporary and pleasant feeling of calm, but this is accomplished by surges of blood sugar followed by blood sugar crashes. Males tend to experience the sugar crash as "the jitters"; females tend to experience depression or feeling low. Boys tend to become impulsive; girls become temporarily withdrawn and distracted.

High-fiber foods, protein, yogurt, and milk (soy milk is as good as or better than cow's milk because it distinctly and quickly builds alerting neurotransmission—what starts us thinking in the morning) are better morning foods. They do not induce a minor serotonin crisis in the body and they build learning ability by helping brain-cell growth more than carbohydrates do. They also help a child stay more awake.

We recommend that preschools and kindergartens ban sugar snacks in the school and in lunch boxes. Sugars and starches also ought to be limited at lunch, as they make the brain groggy, and the child neither learns nor tests as well afterward. If, later in the day, a child is going to engage in athletics, there is some use for higher carbohydrates, but rarely until then.

Fatty Acids

During the preschool and kindergarten years, the brain is forming at a fast pace. Neurotransmission and synaptic processes are forming in patterns that will persist for life. It is important to protect a child's diet throughout life, but early childhood is especially critical in establishing the eating habits that the child will follow.

Brain research has taught us about fatty acids that help brains grow and about problems that other foods create for growing children. Typical Western hemisphere diets (especially children's diets) do not include enough omega-3 fatty acids (the kind found in fish, fish products, and fish oils), and our brains suffer as a result. The lack sets our children up to fail as learners and as well-socialized humans. Although the major problems may not show up until later, they begin in early childhood.

The human brain is just over 60 percent fat and requires omega-3 acids to promote optimal performance. Lack of omega-3 acids is linked to psychiatric and neurological disorders, such as depression, ADHD, learning disorders, and other behavioral disorders. This link continues into adolescence, when bipolar personality disorders and schizophrenia emerge. In the book *Smart Fats,* Michael Schmidt says: "Preliminary studies indicate that an imbalance of essential fatty acid intake may well relate to such problems as social violence, aggressive behavior, and suicide." These occur at lower rates in cultures that intake omega-3s regularly.

The brain does not produce omega-3 fatty acids; they must be eaten to enter the body. Fatty acids are the structural molecules of which nerve endings are made. Human synapses—brain connections—are membranes composed of fatty acids, such as arachidonic acid, docosahexaenoic acid (DHA), and eicosapentaenoic acid (EPA). If the brain doesn't have enough fatty acids, the nerve endings and the synaptic membranes are affected and neurotransmission deteriorates. The shape and constitution of receptors change. If the receptors are nuanced inappropriately for the normal brain process, neurotransmitters such as dopamine and serotonin are affected. Serotonin affects violent, depressive, and impulsive behavior. Dopamine affects everything from mood to motor ticks.

For boys and girls, the lack of fatty acids in their diet can be devastating. Boys become impulsive and aggressive, have problems with motor skills and motor ticks, and suffer learning disorders. Girls develop depression, eating disorders, emotional disturbance, and an increase in the rate of learning disorders.

Special Education

MUCH OF SPECIAL EDUCATION IS FOCUSED ON BOYS, WHO ARE MORE APT TO BE diagnosed as having learning disorders or attention deficits. It is also important to pay close attention to the special educational needs of girls, whose disabilities often are not as marked as boys' and, therefore, can be missed.

A Program for Reading and Writing

The largest group of learning disabilities involves reading and writing—predominantly male deficiencies. Phonemic awareness is crucial to handling reading and writing disabilities, and the computer enhances phonemic awareness through spatial stimulation.

➡ *Fast ForWord*TM: Fast ForWordTM is a series of research-based programs for students with learning disabilities (reading in particular), developed by neuroscientists Paula Tallal and Michael Merzenich. It includes "Fast ForWord Language" (for ages five through twelve), "Fast ForWord Middle and High School" (for adolescents and adults), "Fast ForWord Language to Reading" (used after the "Language" program to help students make the link between spoken and written language, for those up to age sixteen), and "Fast ForWord Reading" (a supplemental program to improve reading skills). Modules consist of interactive computer games that first teach students to distinguish between similar sounds, using artificially slowed speech, and then challenge them gradually to increase their recognition speed.

Preschool and Kindergarten

Most special education and learning disorders occur after age six, and many learning diagnoses are based on cultural expectations. For example, we are relatively obsessed with early reading and label nonreaders as "behind." In Hungary and Sweden, reading is not taught until the age of seven, and children in both countries test high in reading skills in later grades. Because males have a disadvantage in early reading, many in the United States are diagnosed with learning disorders.

The same holds true for behavioral disorders (BD). The United States is far ahead of Europe in BD diagnoses per capita. We medicate earlier than in Europe and use 85 percent of the world's Ritalin. Brain-based gender research and multicultural research show us that a culture's definition of normal development may not be normal for many children.

Some preschoolers and kindergartners do need special help. They, especially, can benefit from our knowledge of how bonding affects their brain development.

Bonding and School-Home Alliances

Bonds, attachment, and supervision give the growing brain the sense of safety and stability it needs to move from being disordered to learning. Many young children with behavioral problems can be helped by a teacher bonding with them and developing positive working relationships with their extended families.

➡ *Behavior-Management Plans:* Carrie Whalley met with the mother of a BD boy and discovered that the mother and father had been separated for a long time, so the boy's life was split between two houses with two sets of expectations, rules, and discipline patterns. Everyone who dealt with the boy at school met with his mother and created a behavioral-management plan. The plan gave him a goal to work toward and rewarded him for doing the right thing (instead of acting out to gain attention). Everyone (including his mother) gave him praise and celebrations for positive behavior. With consistency, his behavior improved.

Use of Psychotropic Medication

Psychotropic medication is prescribed to between one-half and one million children under the age of seven. Prozac tends to be prescribed to girls and Ritalin to boys. Boys, because of naturally low serotonin levels, tend to have problems with impulse (hyperactivity) and, because of brain layout and functioning (less left-hemisphere activity), with attention span. Girls tend to show overt signs of depression but have fewer problems with impulse and attention. Our research indicates that psychotropic medication for children of this age is potentially dangerous, not just to the child but to society. The exceptions are highly violent children and those whose lives seem to be at stake.

Although the rate of depression among this age group is increasing, as well as diagnoses such as ADD and ADHD, we should not be using medication to solve what are mainly attachment, bonding, and brain-based gender issues that are masked by the medication. Many presumed disorder behaviors are actually indications of (1) caregivers' and parents' lack of training in normal child development and (2) cultural pressure to create a uniformity in children that is unnatural. Teachers are often relieved to have a child calmed down or pepped up, but medication interrupts the natural flow of a child's brain development. It allows parents to continue their disengaged parenting styles and it permits the school to continue the trend of warehousing the child, rather than creating one-on-one bonding through (1) more teachers and care providers who stay longer at day care and preschools; (2) better classrooms; (3) engaging lesson plans; (4) teacher training in brain differences; and (5) clear discipline systems and character education.

Children who take psychotropic medicines are more likely to become addicted to drugs and alcohol in later life. They are likely to become medication-dependent and not develop internal psychological coping mechanisms, finding themselves adrift when off the medication.

In the preschool and kindergarten age group, nearly 70 percent of medication is given to boys. This indicates a cultural response to the male brain system. Boys who are medicated at age four, five, or six learn early that they are "sick" or "defective"—labels that stick in the souls of these children.

In this age group, perhaps 90 percent of medicated kids are less loved than they need to be; their brains, therefore, are not developing as gracefully as our culture wants them to. This situation is especially frightening in the United States, where we use more psychotropics on young children than any other country does.

George Will reported on a cross-cultural study of children using and not using drugs, conducted by Ken Jacobson of the University of Massachusetts. Using a grid of thirty-five behaviors (including giggling, blurting out answers, squirming, and tapping fingers), Jacobson found no significant difference in the presence of the behaviors in the diagnosed and undiagnosed groups.

Teachers, parents, and the community are tempted to medicate a child with a temperament that differs from the uniformity that makes the classroom and home "easier." From a neurological point of view, it is through well-balanced diversity that the human species flourishes. We have not thrived by shutting down diverse temperaments, ideas, and ways of succeeding.

One-on-one attention is generally the best antidote for the young child's behavioral and learning ills. A smaller, more structured class; connections to parents and/or grandparents; and connection to a teacher can change the life of a child.

➡ *Nonmedical Options:* Recent studies show success with these nonmedical options:

- Parents and caregivers are educated in normal child development (and typical differences between boys and girls).
- A parent moves from full-time to part-time employment so as to mentor a difficult or spirited child for an additional two or three hours per day.
- The spirited child is moved from the present preschool to a smaller, more intimate one where at least two caregivers or teachers are consistently present.
- The child is led through the day with set routines and discipline systems.
- The child is shown a "stress" area where he can hit a small punching bag or otherwise release energy.
- Alternative medicines are used.

- Grandparents and other concerned caregivers provide new (and nearly daily) support, especially in single-parent homes.
- Talk therapy and counseling augment structural changes in the family and classroom.
- Teachers and parents offer as much art therapy as possible, allowing the child who is in psychological pain to paint or draw when experiencing stress.
- The natural and outdoor world is used more than previously.

Elementary School

Techniques to Encourage Learning

The field of special education, learning disabilities, and behavioral disabilities is one of the fastest growing in education. There are three times as many boys as girls in most special education classrooms, and the majority of diagnosed disorders are related to the male brain because it is not as good at self-development and its growth typically requires external help. Many disabilities that girls experience—which show up less—go unnoticed.

The growing brain develops learning and behavioral disorders when it is stressed because of the breakdown of family and bonding systems, the lack of teacher and parent knowledge of brain development, the increase in environmental overstimulation (from media and other cultural stimulants), and pressure to compete and learn earlier than the brain may be ready to do.

The following are some techniques that can be used in special education:

➡ *Class Within a Class:* In the class-within-a-class program, students are not pulled out for special education programs. The special education teacher goes into the regular classroom and works with all the students. This way, classmates sometimes do not even realize who the special ed students are. All teachers and students can take advantage of the expertise of the special ed teachers, and the special ed students don't have to try to reintegrate into classrooms and make up missed class work.

➡ *Buddy Work and Same-Sex Groupings:* In group work, some students seem to need certain people in the group in order to feel secure in their ability to complete the assignment. Many children like working with a partner of the same sex. In mainstream classrooms, there are many moments for single-sex group work. With special ed students, same-sex partnerships can cut down on brain-learning distractions, making it easier for the brain to go right to the lesson and without navigating gender differences.

➡ *Fewer Words on a Page:* Lois Hedge notes that graphic organizers with short answers or illustrations get boys' attention.

➡ *Helping a Child with Notes and Lists:* One special ed department has self-copying notebook paper. A "buddy" can write his own notes, list, or message down, tear the copies apart, and give one copy to another child (who cannot get them down on paper) to study or take home.

➡ *Spin-the-Wheel Questions:* After reading a story, Jan Miller's students answer comprehension questions from a spin-the-wheel that the children made.

➡ *The Sixty-Second Rule:* When asking a student (especially a boy) to respond verbally, hand over something, or go to a buddy room or recovery room, allow sixty seconds before repeating the request or initiating further action. Usually, within that time, the student will hand over something or leave the room as requested. Behavioral problems may escalate if the teacher demands an immediate response. When the brain is agitated, it requires time to self-stabilize, and the child needs to process issues of saving face, weighing consequences, and managing rage.

➡ *Stress Balls:* Lois lets her students use stress balls. She notes that hyperactive boys seem to need them most.

➡ *Running Errands:* Lois gives a hyperactive child an errand that takes a few minutes. This also builds trust and a sense of responsibility.

➡ *Doing Laps As Discipline:* One teacher has given up taking away recess as discipline, as offenders are usually the ones who needed that active release. She tallies each student's daily violations and assigns a lap around the playground for each violation. The students get to be active, but they don't get to choose how.

➡ *Cool-Down Card:* Students who are sent to another room or are having trouble are asked to fill out a card, in triplicate form. Copies can be sent home and to the principal to keep track of a child's time-outs or problems. This helps keep everyone informed and gives the child responsibility to own his problem and work through it.

Spatial Stimulants, Movement, and Multisensory Approaches

➡ *Movement and Manipulation of Objects:* For all students, using body movement and manipulating objects in space leads to greater learning than just working with words on paper. For special ed students, this can be even truer.

➡ *Acting Out Lessons:* Acting out lessons is very important for special ed. With movement, more of the brain is being used, so students better remember what they do. We are not sure why movement enhances memory. One theory is that perhaps hippocampal activity is involved when the child moves, so the child develops memory.

➡ *Using Bodies to Make Letters:* Children can be helped to learn spelling by using their bodies to physically represent the letters in the alphabet or a word.

➡ *Multisensory Presentation:* Research indicates that putting material on an overhead projector is more effective than just saying it verbally, because a visual and spatial stimulant is added to the verbal. For many special ed boys, this multisensory approach is crucial, especially in first and second grades, where many boys have not developed good verbal skills.

The Multisensory Approach to Reading Problems

The Lindamood-Bell™ method (including "Phoneme Sequencing" and "Visualizing and Verbalizing") is a well-known multisensory reading approach. It works especially well with boys, who have decreased sensory processing in comparison to girls.

When children have reading problems, it is often because the alphabet, phonemes, and other reading units are being taught only visually or only aurally. The multisensory approach asks the child to trace the letters on a letter form so he "feels" the letter in tactile fashion, then listen to it said, see it, say it, and finally talk about how it felt in his throat to say it. This is learning with more than one sense.

Middle School

Factors in the Need for Special Education

Middle school can be a very difficult time for all students, as they have many developmental challenges and much biological energy to deal with. It is especially difficult for students diagnosed as learning or behaviorally disabled, and the number of these has greatly increased. Although it is essential to separate learning-disability diagnoses from so-called behavioral ones, a lot of children (mostly males) become behavioral problems as part of their ego reaction to their learning vulnerability. Brain and gender research tells us that part of the need for special education lies in these factors:

- The human brain is formatted for preindustrial life, not the overstimulation of today. Most brains can adapt to the constant, intense stimulation of modern life, but some cannot.
- The male brain system is more vulnerable to a learning disability because it does not naturally multitask as well as the female's and is not as flexible.
- The male brain and male hormones mix to drive vulnerable and disabled males toward aggressive, uncontrolled, and inappropriate behavior, which adds to the frequency of male BD diagnoses.

- Classrooms and schools favor the female brain and do not understand the male brain, so some normal males are diagnosed LD or BD. Our culture may systematically withhold from boys the approval and love they need.

We must re-evaluate special education to incorporate brain and gender research. There are three times more males than females diagnosed as learning disordered and about ten times more males diagnosed as behaviorally disordered. Many boys diagnosed as BD lack good male role models and are desperate for a male to pay attention to them. They need bonding, love, respect, acceptance, and approval. If they don't get these in healthy ways, they will seek them in other ways. Along with other innovations, special education needs to focus on male brains, male mentors, male role models, and male culture in order to fully assist these young people. When males do not need to act out so much to be noticed and loved, and their neurological weaknesses are better cared for, especially in early school years, many of their weaknesses won't become disorders. Of course, many girls also feel unloved and undirected.

Techniques to Encourage Learning

The following are some techniques suggested by special ed teachers in middle schools:

➡ *Bonding:* Paula Dee Rogers notes the importance of patience and persistence in trying to bond with students who are at risk and difficult to get close to. A teacher with whom a student has bonded may serve as an intermediary in improving the student's relationships with other teachers. Small, incremental improvements make the difference between a child who is lost and one who comes to love learning.

➡ *Structure and Order:* Structure and order are especially important in special ed. For example, the kids take ROTC seriously. It gives them structure, order, boundaries, and identity—especially important for the male students. Ruth Whertvine has noticed a dearth of positive role models for middle school boys and African American boys in particular. She believes that some of ROTC's success with these boys lies in the teacher's presence. It also provides some of them their first real taste of social success.

➡ *Consistent Guidelines and Discipline:* Ruth notes that the boys especially "respond to guidelines that are set and then enforced." This is evident in the ways in which males structure sports, the military, and gangs.

➡ *Lack of Pressure or Blame:* Sometimes a student must be allowed to calm down without any pressure. Often, a calm discussion of behavior, without blame, can elicit some responsibility for the behavior.

➡ *Something to Cuddle:* Linda allows each of her students to keep a Beanie Baby® on his or her desk and to pick it up during class. The boys use them as much as the girls. They seem to be able to listen better if they have something to touch.

➡ *Safe Spaces:* With her severely disabled kids, Ruth has noticed that "Boys enjoy crawling under cabinets to read. They have a need for security that we sometimes forget these boys still need."

➡ *Bulletin Boards:* Ruth mentions the intense need of all the BD students to be noticed. Her students put up their own bulletin boards. Because they take ownership in their work, they do not tear them down. For the first time, many at-risk students have something displayed in school that is theirs. Prone to calling negative attention to themselves in the hope of getting any at all, they enjoy feeling cared about positively.

➡ *Multimedia Slogans:* One teacher handed out slips of paper on which she had written, "You can't get to the mountaintop if you don't climb." Her class made a collage with this saying at the top. Some students added photos; some brought pictures cut out of magazines; and others did their own artwork, both written and visual.

➡ *Missions:* Randall sees many BD and LD boys who are not connected with peer groups. Some walk around, looking dejected, looking at groups of boys. They seek the attention of these groups through aggressive acts and misbehavior. Randall gives such boys missions—series of tasks or sacrifices in order to complete a bigger picture. This also works with girls, but especially with boys who are hungry for a direction and a cause, something to which they can attach their affection.

➡ *Class Within a Class:* Brenda Bock's sixth-grade students are the class-within-a-class learning-disability team. Brenda has found that having the LD students within other classes helps to build confidence in taking learning risks. Anne Walker confirms Brenda's success stories about the class within a class and the use of teams.

➡ *Separate-Sex Learning:* The advantages of single-sex classes double or triple in special education settings. Sara says that kids in single-sex groups work better with one another, get more done, and create fewer distractions.

Shari works mainly with boys. She sees advantages in single-sex classes, not only in the academic and behavioral learning process but also in the deep bonds that can form when there are fewer distractions. With bonding, there are fewer behavioral problems.

➡ *Character Education:* Ruth has discovered that integrating character education into her classes cuts down on behavioral issues. She ritualizes character education into morning mentoring, in the first hour of the day. She focused on one skill per week. Other teachers try to reinforce the skills during regular classes.

The Underachiever

Middle school classrooms are very verbal (left-brain) places, and the level of verbal skill required far surpasses that of a century ago, when much learning was experiential. There is right-brain dominance in many gifted (and many disabled) kids, and we suspect this link in underachievers. The number of underachievers is growing, and a disproportionate number of them are boys. Underachievement may also be caused by depression, learning disabilities, bad time management, excessive time spent with mass media, lack of support for learning at home, and boredom with the process of learning. We hope that underachievement becomes a focus of research, especially in the context of brain patterns.

Teachers who work with underachievers note the following factors in raising underachievers' performance:

- Teacher-student bonding and greater attention to children's emotional needs
- Continual and intense contact between the school and home
- Team learning and group work, even pair work
- More physical movement and experiential learning
- Increasing the competitive aspects of learning: games, contests, puzzles, and debates motivate some underachieving students, especially boys.

High School

Statistically, high school students who express themselves well through spoken and written communication are less likely to be classified as needing special education. The majority of high school students in special education are boys.

Techniques to Encourage Learning

Special ed teachers in Missouri who are trained in brain-based gender research offer the following techniques:

- Increased teaching of problem-solving approaches
- Increased teaching of conflict-resolution skills
- Decreased verbal instruction
- Increased one-on-one mentoring in all classes, especially alternative-education classes
- Increased use of bonding activities between teachers and students and among students
- Allowing more response time for questions

Other teacher-recommended techniques are

➡ *The Sixty-Second Rule:* Many high school students don't need additional time before responding or acting in response to a request, but those in special ed benefit from being allowed increased response time. Waiting before encouraging an answer or calling on someone else makes a major difference in the number and quality of responses, especially from male students.

➡ *Integrating Curricula with the Arts:* The arts are such whole-brain activities, they can work with reading-disabled, generally learning-disabled, behaviorally disabled, and all difficult students.

Frances was producing Shakespeare's plays. One of the toughest, most difficult special ed boys auditioned for Romeo. He wrote a special soliloquy to present before the play began. It set the context for the character and precluded laughter about his costume. He got standing ovations, his behavior changed after that, and he graduated. Frances taught problem students to focus by offering them the attention they wanted.

➡ *Sentenced to the Arts:* Alan Wells, in Kansas City, Missouri, has a program, funded by a grant from the U.S. Department of Justice, that allows juveniles who commit crimes to be ordered to participate in an arts program run by a participating school or agency. Early results are promising.

8

Planning Your Own
Experiential Activities

STUDIES INDICATE THAT PEOPLE LEARN BETTER WHEN THEY ARE ACTIVELY ENGAGED IN what they are learning. Students who are listening to a teacher talking or watching a video are passive receivers rather than active participants. When one is "doing," one is using more of oneself to learn.

Introducing Experiential Learning

One of the strengths of learning-by-doing is that as the student becomes involved with the lesson, he or she is more likely to internalize it, so it is less likely to be perceived as someone else's (the teacher's) content. As students engage in activities and relate to them, they are more apt to ask questions, make inferences, and so on.

Many experiential activities in the classroom involve pairs, trios, and group work. The safety of the group helps more hesitant students to verbalize their reactions, understandings, and conclusions. Group work also allows students to experience, observe, and learn about group process and group dynamics, including listening, cooperating, and competing.

At the conclusion of the activity, the teacher can ask a series of questions designed to elicit learning from the students. In this way, they learn from one another's outcomes, feelings, and insights. The new learning is retained best if students have opportunities to practice their new skills or talk about their new knowledge soon after the learning experience. They may receive coaching-type feedback on their approaches or skills. Then additional content can be added to round out the lesson. Students also can be helped to understand how their learning might be used in the "real world."

The following describes this process in more detail.

The Natural Learning Process

Of course, any human activity can be a basis for experiential learning, but the term usually is applied to structured tasks, games, role plays, experiments, and other activities that have specific learning objectives. What makes this approach different is that students derive their learning from their experiences, rather than merely reading or hearing about something.

One of the bonus lessons in this type of activity can be "learning how to learn." When students understand the natural learning process, they can begin to view all experiences—even those with negative outcomes—as learning opportunities, rather than as random events with no meaning or as "failures." By developing skills in observing, reflecting, generalizing, analyzing, and planning future actions, children become not just learners of a particular topic but students of life.

There is a natural cycle that humans engage in when learning something. To be most effective, every experiential learning activity should allow for all stages of this cycle to be completed. These stages are listed below. The amount of time required for each depends on the nature of the experience, the depth of the intended lesson, the age and sophistication of the students, and various other factors.

1. *Experiencing* an interaction, activity, game, task, role play, questionnaire, and so forth, in which ideas, insights, feelings, and so on are generated. By engaging in the experience together, students have a shared basis for observation and experimentation.

During the subsequent discussions, they may find that they have different reactions to or insights from the activity. This enriches the learning experience for all and teaches another valuable lesson: that not everybody experiences things or sees things the same way. However, the discussion of what tends to happen in such activities helps to point toward generalized patterns that lead to the overall learning.

In this and the following stages, the teacher can write important rules, procedures, questions, lists, discussion points, and insights on a board or newsprint pad. The newsprint can be posted in the room to help students remember the materials.

2. *Talking about feelings and reactions* to the experience. Especially if the planned activity is likely to generate emotive responses, each student, in turn, is asked to talk briefly about how he or she felt during the activity—how he or she reacted to what happened. It is difficult to learn cognitively when feelings have not been dealt with. By processing this information first, students also are helped to understand that their emotional and historic ways of responding to situations and events may color what they extract from them. This also lets students hear others' reactions, which may be different from their own. If the class is large, pairs or subgroups can be formed for the sharing, with generalized reports subsequently made to the total class.

3. *Asking "What happened?"* The teacher initiates a student discussion of what actually happened during, and as a result of, the activity. Now the emphasis is on interactions, dynamics, general behaviors, patterns, and outcomes that occurred during the activity. Depending on the purpose of the lesson and the nature of the activity, the "what happened" may be physical (the result of a physical task or experiment) or relational (the result of an interpersonal exchange, group dynamic, or competitive or collaborative task). Subgroups can be formed to discuss different aspects of the activity and then report out to the total class.

4. *Identifying what tends to happen in general.* Now it is time to generalize the behaviors, patterns, and dynamics in terms of other possible situations, as in "If such-and-such happens, people tend to such-and-such." Students can be asked to state the typical effects of the identified behaviors, interactions, patterns, and so on in "real life" situations. This stage is a transfer from experience to learning. When students have volunteered what they can in this regard, the teacher can add more examples, if necessary. Students can be encouraged to make notes at this point of what they want to remember, from their own insights and those expressed by others, and of things they might want to practice. If appropriate, subgroups can be given the task of listing how the insights or new skills might relate to a particular problem or

situation that is being considered by the class. (This can be an historic situation or one in literature.)

5. *Answering the "So what?"* Students now are asked to consider how their new insights, knowledge, or skills could be used. They (or pairs or subgroups) may be asked to describe situations, make lists, or develop guides that show their understanding of the learnings to be applied. When students see a possible use for what they have learned, they are more likely to remember it. The teacher may round out this stage by adding possible applications or by adding to the lesson with a brief oral presentation, a visual model, or a short videotape related to the topics the students have discussed.

6. *Planning to use the learning.* With more mature boys and girls, if the lesson is important enough to the class, the teacher can help students to cement their learning by asking them to identify specific ways in which they will use their new knowledge or skills in real situations. (This may not be necessary or possible with younger students and certain topics.) Students can plan their applications individually or in helping pairs or small groups. It may be done with the aid of worksheets. Girls may prefer writing their plans; boys may prefer constructing models, diagrams, or flow charts.

The students should be directed to make their application plans as specific as possible, so that they can assess the effectiveness of their actual application "experiments" (that is, the possible situation, the persons involved, when it will be done, the specific behaviors to be done or skills to be used, the goals of the planned behavior, and possible ways of getting feedback on its effectiveness).

If the class has bonded, students may be asked to volunteer to describe their plans. (Some students may wish to share their plans only with a "buddy" or trusted teacher.) Practice sessions, such as role plays and controlled experiments, can allow students to try out behaviors or approaches and receive feedback in a relatively safe environment. Students may form partnerships or small groups to reinforce one another's progress toward planned applications.

If the topic is important or related to a larger lesson, the students can be given homework that asks them to apply their learning in other hypothetical situations. Depending on the topic and class, they may be asked to report back on their results.

The students should be made aware that not all applications—which are basically experiments—will "work" as envisioned. If boys and girls can learn to view their attempts (at interacting, acting, cooking, drawing, sports activities, and so on) as experiments, they are less likely to be deterred from trying to learn from those experiences, regroup, and try again. This is especially important for less confident girls and boys.

The Teacher as Facilitator

One aspect of learning is that what one individual takes from an experience may be slightly or greatly different from what another derives from the experience. In processing any experiential activity, it is important that the teacher ask what the students learned, validate their experiences, and not brush aside any child's feelings or insights as "wrong." The teacher then can say "And . . ." to take it further or point out other learning possibilities. The teacher can direct the focus in the desired direction by saying something like: "That's very interesting, Jeff, and somebody might also. . . ." "This shows us that different people see various aspects of a situation/sides of an issue differently." "Are there any other observations about this?" "Did anyone notice anything else about this?" It is important that the students be charged with coming up with the initial observations, not allowed to rely on the teacher to tell them what they got from the experience.

Feedback should be given in a coaching manner, so that students can receive it without defensiveness, and in an amount that they can handle and remember.

The natural learning cycle includes applying one's new knowledge or skills (experimenting with them) and receiving feedback—from individuals or the environment; modifying the behavior, if necessary; and trying again until the desired effect is obtained.

It is important that teachers help students to view each attempt to apply a skill or knowledge as an experiment—a new experience to be analyzed and learned from—rather than becoming embarrassed or frustrated with perceived "failures." One of the main lessons to be learned through this cycle is that life is an ongoing series of lessons, and that we are continually experiencing, extracting meaning from our experiences, applying our insights, testing them, and modifying them (as necessary) in order to become more effective. Sometimes, what we learn is that we cannot "make" something happen. Each new experience, each new attempt, is the start of another cycle. Noticing one's reactions to an experience, thinking about what happened and then what tends to happen in similar situations, identifying generalized patterns and principles, thinking about how the resulting insights can be used to obtain desired outcomes, and trying out new approaches or behaviors is the natural process of life-long learning.

With older students, it may be pointed out that this is also a basis of scientific inquiry and discovery. Historic discoveries can be described and further experiments can be planned from this perspective.

Experiential Learning Techniques

Experiential learning activities should be selected to suit the lesson and the particular group of students. Some typical structured learning techniques are as follows:

1. Younger children can learn from playing games and carrying out simple tasks or sets of activities. They also learn from unstructured play and experiments, such as with water tables, sand, and magnets.

2. Lecturing is often used to present theories and content, but students may perceive this content as being more important to the teacher than to them. The trick is to find some way to reinforce the lecture so that it has meaning for the student. The teacher can initiate a discussion of what the content might mean in terms of the students' lives or in our present society, or the presentation may be reinforced by using another technique, such as experimentation, drama, role playing, art, a "fishbowl" discussion, and so on.

3. Structured activities can be used to engage visual, auditory, tactile, emotional, and cognitive aspects of learning as well as to initiate discussion. They provide the opportunity for experimentation, exploration, and practice of the concepts underlying a lecture, reading, or other input. A structured activity is not complete in itself; it should be followed by a discussion of what happened, what that might mean, and the possible uses of the students' new insights or skills. This discussion should be elicited from the students, with general guidance by the teacher.

Typical structured activities include

- Verbal communication (for example, the "Rumor" or "Gossip" game, passing along instructions for completing a task, expressing feelings,

explaining something, self-disclosure, practicing assertion, con-
fronting, practicing empathic responses)
- Information sharing (for example, in solving a puzzle, mystery, or
  problem)
- Transactions (for example, choosing, resource sharing, negotiating,
  bargaining)
- Fantasy (guided imagination journeys)
- Nonverbal communication (for example, charades or pantomime;
  illustrating the difficulty of communicating without a common
  language)
- Competition and/or collaboration tasks (and comparison of the two)
- Construction tasks (for example, using blocks, straws, Lego® blocks,
  Tinkertoy® pieces, or Erector Set® pieces to build buildings or bridges)

- Model making (a variety of media are available)
- Creating art objects (a variety of media are available)
- Problem definition and problem solving (real or fictional)
- Task completion (for example, writing, passing a baton, throwing a ball to the beat of music, blindfold activities, planning, designing)
- Games (these vary in structure and complexity, but most include situations, rules, objectives, active involvement, competition and/or cooperation, and payoffs). *Primary Games,* by Steve and Kim Sugar, tells how to select and use experiential learning games in teaching grades K–8 and includes instructions for twenty-five original games.
- Puzzles (for example, the Chinese Tangram, word puzzles, math puzzles, information-sharing puzzles)

4. Role playing, in which two or more students interact based on a given scenario, provides an opportunity to practice effective behaviors in a safe environment. Role playing allows students to practice desired behaviors, try out new behaviors and approaches, examine a situation, and put themselves on the "other side" of an issue to create insight into the motivations and roles of others. Some role plays are structured (with prewritten characters and scripts), and some are unstructured (students are told of a situation and directed to play themselves). For some purposes, role plays are based on situations in the students' lives, so that they can practice ways of dealing with them. Other students and the teacher can give feedback after each role play, as appropriate. When role plays enact historic or literary events, they allow students to explore the pertinent issues and to imagine what it may have been like for the characters involved.

5. Questionnaires and other types of feedback forms that are filled in by students can provide information for a variety of purposes. Students tend to be more interested in information that is about them, and it is difficult to argue with information that one has supplied. Some questionnaires can be used to open up a further lesson, and some can be developed by the students. When students themselves tally the responses, they can see where the information comes from, how it is organized, and how the results are derived.

6. In high school classes, the students are mature enough to work with modified case studies in order to practice problem solving, decision making,

conflict resolution, and so on, in "real-life situations." This is analogous to lab experiments in science classes. Taking on a situation and attempting to resolve it or deal with it helps students develop a range of skills. The description of the situation should contain all the data the students need but not suggested solutions. It may include people's feelings about the situation as well as their past behaviors. The students' task is to apply skills that they have learned. When cases are acted out, they become more like role playing.

Important Factors in Planning Experiential Learning

Some important things to consider when planning an experiential learning activity are as follows:

Purpose(s)

Identify realistic, specific outcomes that you want to occur as a result of the activity. Remember that you can "introduce . . .," "allow students to experience . . .," "help students to practice . . .," "explore . . .," and so on, but you can only guide, not dictate, what they will actually derive from the experience. The experience itself should be selected or designed to facilitate the achievement of the desired outcomes.

Students

Consider the following:

1. Who are the students?
2. What is their maturity level and readiness level in respect to the topic?
3. What is their familiarity with this type of activity?
4. What is their familiarity with or relationship to one another?
5. What is the level of trust in the group?
6. What preparation have they received for this?

Timing

It is important to plan so that adequate time is available to complete as much of the natural learning process as is appropriate for the age level of the students, the topic, and the complexity of the activity. Plan some time for unanticipated delays or discussions.

Involvement

Each student should have something to do during the activity. This may be actively doing a task, responding to or scoring a questionnaire, communicating, listening, purposefully observing others (perhaps taking notes), discussing feelings or ideas, analyzing something, making lists or writing action plans, and so on.

The use of "observers," who have prepared observation forms with specific things to be noted, can enhance many experiences, such as interactions, negotiations, problem-solving sessions, and role plays. Having the observers report on their observations should be structured into the activity.

Preferred Input Modes

Some research indicates that there are three primary ways in which humans input data from their environments. Some children best remember what they see (many girls); some best remember what they hear; and some best remember what they experience physically (especially many boys). In order to make learning memorable for all types of learners, it is a good idea to build visual experiences and/or visual aids, talking and listening, and some physical activity into each lesson.

Visual aids include printed materials, posters and other artwork, overhead transparencies, videotapes, activities that involve visual images, note taking, and listing important points or discussion outcomes on a board during lectures or discussions.

Talking and listening include brief lectures, audiotapes, activities that involve communication with others, practice in active listening, discussions (in pairs, small groups, or the total class), and reporting.

Physical activity includes using the body, moving, and manipulating objects and can be built into many lessons. Making notations and creating charts, diagrams, and models also are quasi-physical activities. Physical senses and feelings also can provide physical learning for many children.

Instructions

Instructions to students regarding the initial activity and any subsequent work (scoring, group discussions, reporting, and so on) must be clear. Simple instructions may be given verbally; activity rules and instructions for, say, assembling something, may also be given as handouts or posted where all can see them.

Modes of Expression

Children vary in their ability to express themselves, and some children are more willing than others to share their feelings and experiences verbally. Typically, girls find both easier to do than boys. Drawing, making collages, miming, singing, writing poetry, acting, and other means of expression may help some children to reflect on and share their feelings, ideas, and insights.

Psychological Safety

The classroom should be a "safe" place where new ideas, skills, and behaviors can be "tried on." In discussing experiential learning, children should be encouraged to be open to new ideas, nonjudgmental, and sensitive. It is important for the teacher to model these norms.

Equipment, Manipulatives, and Props

Some activities require no equipment, some require only things that are found in the typical classroom, and some require extra props or preparation. Basic materials include blank paper, pencils, a chalkboard and chalk or a white board and markers, a newsprint pad on an easel and felt-tipped markers, and masking tape. Other typical materials are paper, scissors, crayons, colored markers, blindfolds, building blocks, puzzle or game pieces, and construction materials.

Planning Activities and Games to Enhance Learning

The following checklist may be of help in planning your own learning activities:

1. Purpose
   - Intended benefits/outcomes/learnings
2. Students to Be Involved
   - Age(s)
   - Number of students
   - Readiness level
   - Ability to observe, infer, analyze, deduce, discuss
   - Preparation needed
3. How to Structure the Activity
   - Type of activity
   - Stages of activity
   - Preparation needed
4. Time Required
   - For transportation (if applicable)
   - For introduction to the activity and mental setup
   - For physical setup
   - For the primary activity
   - For sharing of feelings, analysis, and discussions
   - For group discussion and reporting
   - For action planning
   - For reporting (at the time of the activity or later)
5. Resources Needed
   - Space (area, size, and type of space)
   - Materials (audiovisual equipment, other types of equipment, props, manipulatives, sunscreen, water, and so forth)
   - Transportation
   - Financing
   - Other

6. Who Else Is Involved
   - Cooperation needed (from other teachers, parents, representatives of venue, presenters, guides, and others)
   - Advance permission needed (from administration, parents, and others)
   - Necessary prior arrangements, reservations, and so forth
7. How to Facilitate
   - How to help children process what happens and what they are learning (for example, questioning, pair or small-group discussions, class discussions)
   - How to help children represent and express their feelings
   - How to help children represent and express their learnings
   - How children will represent their planned uses of new knowledge (for example, the possible situation, the possible persons involved, when it will be done, the specific behaviors to be done or skills to be used, the goals of the planned behavior or application, and possible ways of receiving feedback on its effectiveness)

Developmental Themes for Creating Learning Techniques and Activities

Following are listings of developmental themes that occur in this guide. They are intended to serve as taking-off points for developing classroom techniques, games, experiential learning activities, and similar innovations.

First are themes that appear at all grade levels. An example is "bonding and attachment," with the subcategories of "caring teachers," "parental involvement," and "mentors and role models." These are needed by every growing child's brain and psyche. These general themes are not repeated under the listings for the different school levels unless they are uniquely relevant to learning for children of that age group or unless they are followed by sublistings that are.

Of course, the apparent "categories" of listings aren't finite; there is a great deal of overlap. Some are based on teaching modality and some are based on content. For example, "variety in teaching modalities," "multisensory input," "using manipulatives," and "movement" can apply to teaching language arts, social science, math, science, art, and other classes. Again, the intent is not to categorize as much as it is to spark ideas for a variety of teaching techniques and activities that can enrich classroom learning for both boys and girls.

All School Levels

- Bonding and attachment
    - Caring teachers
    - Parental involvement
    - Mentors and role models
- Rite-of-passage experiences
- Gender differences
    - Accommodating deductive and inductive reasoning
    - Movement necessary for boys' learning
    - Same-sex learning groups
- Dealing with aggression
    - Aggression nurturance
    - Empathy nurturance
- Stress-release techniques
    - Verbalizing feelings—especially for boys
    - Healthy physical ways to release stress
- Language skills
    - Communication
        - Positive feedback
        - Assertion
            - Using "I" statements
        - Verbalizing feelings and preferences
        - Negotiation
        - Conflict-resolution techniques
- Problem solving
- Group and pair learning
- Variety in teaching media and modalities
    - Making math less abstract for girls
    - Multisensory stimulation
    - Whole-brain activities
        - Games and puzzles
        - Music

> Using manipulatives
>> Increasing spatial learning—especially for girls

- Nutrition
- Physical activity for health
   Physical learning
- The outdoor, natural world

Preschool and Kindergarten

- Bonding and attachment rituals
- Routines and schedules
- Communication
   Increasing empathy nurturance and verbalization
   Verbalizing feelings
      Using "I" statements
   Giving positive feedback to others
- Healthy aggression play
   Cause and effect
- Movement
   Climbing
   Building activities
- Self-directed activities
- Manipulatives
   Developing fine motor skills
- The outdoor, natural world
   Walks
- Continuums

Elementary School

- Movement
   Developing motor skills
   Movement songs and games
   Sports
- Variety in teaching media and modalities
   Multisensory stimulation
      Seeing, feeling, and hearing new words
      Storytelling
      Acting

Manipulatives

Making math concrete

Experiments

- Language skills

Communication

Identifying and verbalizing feelings and problems

Using "I" statements

Responding

Using nonverbal communication

Reading

Writing

Graphic organizers

- Dealing with stress and conflict

Writing about feelings and problems

Drawing

Anger management

Cause and effect

Peer respect

Switching sides, exchanges

Mediation

- Motivation

Extra encouragement for girls

- Character and values

Media influences

Cooperation and competition

Healthy competition

- Group work

Buddy work

Cooperative learning groups

Learning about group dynamics

- The outdoor, natural world

Gardening

Middle School

- Building self-esteem

Biographical material

       Rite-of-passage experiences

       Showcasing girls

- Psychosocial education

       Social skills

       Gender education

       Sexual ethics

       Peer respect, kudos

          Peer dilemmas

       Discussions, fishbowls, questioning

- Character and values
- Cooperative learning groups and pairs

       Exploring group dynamics

       Team building

- Same-sex learning groups
- Stress-release techniques
- Writing

       Note taking

       Graphic organizers

- Variety in teaching media and modalities

       Multisensory learning

          Role playing

       Scholarly discourse

       Seminars

- The outdoor, natural world

       Field trips

          Writing and drawing in nature

       Participation in ecology/conservation-oriented activities

- Physical movement

       Sports and athletics

- Real-life applications
- Understanding deductive and inductive reasoning

High School

- Self-image and self-respect
- Psychosocial learning

       Consideration and respect for peers

          Peer dilemmas

Gender differences
Fishbowl discussions
Sexual education and ethics
- Character and values
- Communication
Verbalizing feelings and stresses
Talking about problems
Assertion
Apologizing
Questioning
Understanding others' nonverbal communication
- Mediation
- Comparing competition and collaboration
- Stress-management techniques
- Managing aggression
- "Ropes" activities
- Group work
Exploring and utilizing group dynamics
- Variety in teaching media and modalities
Multisensory learning
Journaling, note taking
Manipulatives
Role playing and reenacting
Using visual and auditory media
Creating plays, movies, revues
Music and raps
Case studies
Experiments
Invention
Research projects
Art
- The outdoor, natural world
Field trips
Participation in ecological/conservation programs

Structural Innovations

GENDER-SPECIFIC INNOVATIONS ARE EASIER TO IMPLEMENT WHEN MAJOR STRUCTURAL innovations are in place.

Preschool and Kindergarten

Innovations to Encourage Learning

Our research suggests the following things that preschool and kindergarten teachers can do to facilitate learning in boys and girls. Four are key during these years:

1. One-on-one lessons between teachers and students
2. A strong use of group work among students, especially the self-motivated
3. Use of manipulatives and interaction with the physical environment for nearly every lesson
4. A delicate balance between teacher interpretation of lessons for the student and uninterpreted student free play

Because girls tend to mature in many verbal skills earlier than boys, they often can be taught certain things earlier, especially if the teacher likes to use lots of words and instruction. Boys stand a better chance of learning at the same time as girls do if the teacher de-emphasizes verbal instruction; uses graphs, charts, and manipulatives; rethinks the use of space and movement in the class; and employs group work.

Parent-Involvement Programs

It is immensely important that school and family life be connected. Research indicates that there are "windows of opportunity" during the early years of a child's life when learning takes place more easily. If brain development is well-accomplished at home in the early years of a child's life, the brain is ready to learn when the child enters school.

➡ *The Parents as Teachers Program:* In collaboration with a team of neuroscientists from Washington University School of Medicine in St. Louis, the Parents as Teachers (PAT) National Center developed a comprehensive neuroscience-enriched curriculum to help parents of preschool children understand what to expect during each stage of a child's development. Through a network of local programs, PAT develops curriculum and trains and certifies parent educators to visit homes and work with parents to provide them with parenting support and information on the developmental needs of their infants and toddlers. The program also includes group meetings, developmental screenings, and linkages to a network of community resources. PAT-certified parent educators offer parents practical ways to encourage learning, manage challenging behavior, and promote strong parent-child relationships. We recommend this program for all school districts interested in expanding early-childhood learning.

➡ *The Parent Education Coordinator:* Many parents of young children are not trained in brain development and gender-specific development, nor are they supported by family elders. To support them, it is crucial that each school district assign a parent education coordinator to disseminate educational materials, teach parents (by newsletter and workshops) how to provide good discipline, answer parents' questions, offer books and other materials that chart normal child growth, and teach parents about boys' and girls' specific gender needs.

This position might cost a school district an additional teacher's salary, but it pays for itself by cutting down on litigation by parents who feel disconnected with schools because of a communication breakdown or problem with their child. By educating parents and connecting with them, the parent education coordinator becomes an invaluable link between parents and the school.

Elementary School

Use of School Time

The human brain seeks a certain kind of learning schedule. Research reveals that specific areas are of great importance in improving our children's elementary learning.

YEAR-ROUND SCHOOLING The current emphasis on testing creates added pressure on students and curricula. In many countries, students score higher on tests, and they have year-round schooling, with three breaks of three to four weeks each. In the past, children helped with summer chores. This generally is not true now, and the summer school vacation is a concern for many working parents. Teachers have to spend September reteaching things the students have forgotten.

Brain-based research provides good reasons for year-round schooling, particularly between the fourth and sixth grades. This is a crucial time when the brain retains what is used and loses what is not, and summer vacations cut down on retention.

TIMING OF THE SCHOOL DAY If children's caregivers work, we worry about the children's care between the end of school and when the adults return from work. Most juvenile crime, delinquent behavior, and sexual activity among minors occur in this time.

As schools are required to teach more material each year and are asked to add character education, homework done in school hours, study halls, computer training, and so on, a 9:00 to 2:30 school day is less effective, especially for students in the higher grades. The solution is a school day from 8:30 to 3:30. Once the logic is understood by legislators, commensurate pay increases for teachers should follow.

Class Size and Number of Teachers

With one teacher, no more than fifteen students should be in a classroom that is not self-directing. The fifteen brains do not get enough one-on-one attention in an instruction-oriented classroom. This is especially difficult for boys' brains during the early elementary years because of their greater need for environmental stimulation to grow cortical areas. With more students, it is difficult for the teacher and students unless a second teacher or parent volunteer is an important presence. A learning brain that experiences the presence of more than one teacher in a second-grade classroom for at least part of the day enjoys more neurological variety in learning and experience. This is optimal for that age brain. A second teacher, intern, or volunteer should be present in first through third grade, for at least part of the day. By sixth grade, variety is less essential for learning a specific subject. However, depending on class size, a second adult presence (a volunteer) for part of the day may be equally valuable in helping to manage psychosocial energy so that bonding, order, and discipline are improved.

If self-directed lessons are the norm (that is, a Montessori-type classroom), the teacher-student ratio can increase, but volunteers are still necessary for part of the day. Vertical mentoring is also useful in keeping teacher-student ratios healthy (for example, when a sixth-grader consistently comes in to tutor a first-grader).

For the sake of bonding and attachment (on which learning depends), students should have the same teacher all day. A well-respected teacher who keeps the same class all day has fewer discipline problems than are present when students move between classrooms every hour.

Even in the fifth and sixth grades, it is best if students stay in one classroom all day (an environment with which they are bonded with the teacher and one another) and have specialty-subject teachers come into that classroom for an hour or two during the day. Of course, certain classes, such as labs, gym, and art, have to occur outside this classroom.

The advantages of a daylong bonding community are as much neurological as social. Students, particularly those who have difficulty learning, have a consistent community and environment. Problems that emerge for any students have to be worked out, by means of which maturity increases. Healthy conflict emerges when students are continually together under the guidance of respected mentors.

Use of Group Dynamics and Group Work

Especially in elementary school, education is a group process more than an individual one; brain development and social development are intertwined. Individuation is a lower priority; often, the brain is not yet able to act alone. The brain learns because it is part of group learning. It depends on the group for help in processing as well as for reflection on what it is accomplishing. The more projects that groups of two, three, or four students can accomplish together, the more varied the learning experience. This is crucial for both boys and girls.

Of the innovations that follow, many that help boys also help girls and vice versa.

➡ *Cooperative Learning:* Cooperative projects stimulate an elementary student's brain and development. Their impact on problem students is often immeasurable.

Julie Ogilvie's students work on defining the character traits their school has adopted. The students work in cooperative groups and write down what

they think the words mean. Then all students share their ideas. The class makes virtue posters that are hung around the room. Cooperative group activities (such as exhibits and putting on plays) help with community and relationship building.

➡ *Competitive Learning:* Competition also helps the brain. Many teachers use games and contests. They keep kids from being bored, and the rowdiness that can happen is pretty manageable. It is important for kids to notice that life isn't fair all the time and that hard work is required for success.

Competition is natural to the male brain. In Linda Andrews' class, even bored and belligerent boys respond well to games. Linda discovered that girls can benefit from healthy competitive learning, too. In a math game in another third-grade class, students have to see who can calculate the answer fastest. The class says "Congratulations!" to the winner. All the kids like the competition; it's part of "group spirit," and they're not interested in who's bad at something. The teacher structures games so that everyone wins at least a few times.

➡ *Multigenerational Classrooms:* Older students in multigenerational classrooms learn by teaching younger students, and they mature through the responsibility. Younger students benefit from these mentors, and they learn together. The human brain loves the stimulation not only of a teacher but also of multigenerational peers who can help provide order, challenge, wisdom, direction, and intellectual focus. In Montessori classrooms, first grade through third grade learn together, as do fourth through sixth.

➡ *Teaching Teams and Teacher-to-Teacher Support.* In teaching teams, the teachers meet in the morning to plan the day. They visit one another's classrooms frequently (for sharing information and ideas, for observation, and for other reasons). Parents are included, and the school is a community in which teachers and students work together.

Standardized Testing

Legislators nationwide have mandated standardized testing for third, fourth, and sixth grades. Teachers and students put lessons and homework aside for weeks to prepare for these tests. School personnel have been involved in cheating scandals. Pressure is put on children, parents, and educators. This is not healthy for the learning brain.

Legislators have not consulted brain-development research, and standardization should be more flexible than it is. The sheer variety in brain development and capacity among ten-year-olds, for example, makes present standardization an impediment to learning, a terrible drain on teachers and administrators, and an illusory standard of success for parents.

Educators need to instruct legislators about brain development. Ultimately, we hope that these tests can be limited to two grades in elementary school and one in middle school, augmented by the PSAT and SAT in high school.

Middle School

Separate-Sex Education

At least half of middle school learning and discipline problems would be removed if schools were single-sex institutions.

Boys begin puberty with high doses of testosterone. Over just a few years, they need to learn to manage up to twenty times as much of this sex-and-aggression hormone as females. They often find themselves angry, aggressive, awkward, unable to verbalize feelings, focused on girls but afraid of them, competing against boys for girls' attention, and unable to verbally discern the complexities of their developing natures.

Girls begin puberty with high does of progesterone, estrogen, and prolactin, in an even more complicated hormonal condition than boys, and require a stretch of years to learn to manage their new bodies and minds. They experience swings of mood and self-confidence, hyperattention to how they fit in with other girls, and competition for boys' attention. They are often chagrined at how immature boys are. They mask their real selves in order to find "romance." They are harassed, often by boys, about their breast size, height, weight, and other physical characteristics.

Children going through cognitive and physical transformations are likely to pick extreme behaviors as masking devices. Their reactions—from pathology (eating disorders and violent behavior) to simple behavioral adjustments ("dumbing down," not raising their hands or always raising their hands, dominating discussions and being undisciplined to get attention)—affect their learning.

Many ancestral cultures separated boys and girls for a few years just before and during puberty. This accommodated their natural transformations and created gender-safe, mentored environments in which they were taught how to relate to one another, mature, manage themselves, and be of service to others. Even a few decades ago, children developed along gender-specific paths, and marriages were based on social conventions more than on hormonal urges.

Many cultural and familial safeguards for young teenagers no longer exist. Romantic expectations dominate young people. The media force early sexualization on children, and there is greater competition between genders. Boys and girls are thrown together with little supervision and expected to figure out how to accommodate their differences, how and when to mate, what work to pursue, how to develop codes of conduct, how to compete without offending the person one may want to mate with, and so on. They experience gender and role confusion, sexual harassment, early pregnancy, loss of intellectual and academic opportunity, and increased psychosocial stress.

There are more conflicts when the genders are mixed. Peer pressure and social competitiveness, primary tools for socialization of an early adolescent into a toughened adult, are stronger. Some males are lost in competition with females in verbal learning, and girls suffer in comparison with boys in spatial, higher math, and science skills. Classrooms are less disciplined than they should be, and learning quality and academic achievement suffer.

In single-sex classes, competition between the sexes is avoided, and many psychosocial stresses—especially culturally imposed ones—are removed. Test scores and grades are rising in single-sex classrooms and groupings. Kids are less distracted. Teachers report fewer discipline problems and more participation from students, often girls, who were hidden in coed classrooms.

Research shows improvements for girls in girls-only schools and classes, especially in math and science. In classes by themselves, girls are better able to concentrate; they seem more focused. As they work together, self-confidence increases and they learn to manage their transformations.

When boys work only with boys, there are similar improvements in reading, writing, and discipline. The boys work much better together and help one another more, and there are fewer discipline problems. They learn self-management and find safety in working with others who understand them. They are less self-conscious and less potentially destructive in their physical movements when surrounded by other boys.

Teachers can use separate-sex groups in class. When boys and girls seat themselves, a natural segregation often occurs.

We can continue to teach middle school children about life coeducationally in families, religious venues, the media, and elsewhere and offer them gender-specific schools in which to learn the academic skills they will need in life. The school can be relatively free of the gender stresses they encounter elsewhere, well-mentored, and focused on learning. The child then has the best of both worlds.

➡ *Separate-Sex Groups in Class:* Darla Novick gave a lesson on endangered species in which she divided the class into separate-sex groups. The boys were to be loggers who cut down trees. The girls were conservationists, trying to save the spotted owl and its habitat. The boys had similar ideas and so did the girls, but they differed from each other, so if the genders had been mixed, the activity would not have been as successful.

Shawna Middletree has boys on one side of her classroom and girls on the other. When the class was reading *Island of the Blue Dolphins,* she asked students to raise their hands if they believed that it was better to seek risks in life than be safe. All but one male student raised a hand; not one girl did. The class discussed this, and it led to interesting gender and psychosocial teaching.

Separate-sex groupings also can be used to play games, work on projects, prepare reports, and so on.

Psychosocial Education

Middle school students request and benefit from psychosocial education, such as the following:

➡ *Emotional Literacy:* Teach and integrate emotional literacy and emotional development curricula in all courses, not just human growth and development class.

➡ *Sexual Ethics:* Teach sexual ethics curricula in all applicable courses, including physical education (where boys, especially after physical movement, often can be honest and attentive about links between emotional and sexual feelings).

Rites of Passage

The school-based rite of passage is an important component of the classroom, given the hormonal and brain changes in the middle school child. The growing brain needs to mark its progress. Rites of passage provide this, in somewhat different ways for each gender.

It is important for schools to recognize students in some way for different accomplishments. Students who do not achieve recognition for academics and attendance are the ones who need recognition the most. Every child can excel at something (academics, attendance, sports, creativity, sharing, helping, and so on). Generic awards, such as pins, do not reveal whether they are earned for band or basketball or good attendance, so everyone can fit in.

Here are some rites we suggest:

➡ *Introductions, Expectations, and Achievements:* In the first month of the first year of school, have each student stand, show a picture of himself or herself, and talk about the person he or she was, wants to be during the school year, and hopes to be in the future. Have each student also discuss his or her view of what a man or woman is. Make sure each student delineates the kind of help he or she thinks will be needed in the classroom in the current year in order to become a mature young man or woman.

Do this again at the end of the year, directing the monologue toward what has been accomplished and what lies ahead.

In the first month of the next school year, repeat the process. Remember that it takes time for students to write their speeches and feel comfortable with others in the class.

At the end of middle school, have each student show a scrapbook of photos and other items, collected over the middle school years, and discuss them before the whole class or in smaller groups.

➡ *Telling and Showing One's Story:* Lakeview Middle School has each student prepare, in writing or art work, an autobiography of his or her family tree, philosophy of life, and future projections. During the first week of school, each student brings a lunch-sized paper bag filled with anything that represents the student's life and presents these objects to the class. Even problem kids take this seriously. Kids are so hungry for the experience of speaking their own truth, experiencing their own power, knowing themselves, and being noticed for who they are that they make a rite of passage a success for everyone.

➡ *Farewell Letters:* At the end of middle school, have each student write a farewell letter to a classmate or staff member who has meant a great deal to him or her.

➡ *Ropes Courses:* Well-structured "ropes" challenge courses provide opportunities for a rite of passage. Such courses encourage team building, cooperation, communication, and listening skills. Students often are put into groups with students they do not know. At first, boys are not enthusiastic about the get-acquainted activities and are unsure of their fellow group members. Over time, they build up trust and complete activities in which a calculated risk is involved. When the teacher participates with them, the students are amazed that they can develop mutual trust with a teacher, and it is a good bonding experience. It also is a positive risk-taking chance, a rite of passage especially valued by boys.

Such courses exist throughout the country. Some focus on creating rites of passage for troubled youth, who already are prone to high-risk activities. The courses redirect them toward organized risk-taking activities.

Uniforms and Dress Codes

The brain needs orderliness in order to learn. Although some students learn well in nearly any setting, many middle school students, moving through tumultuous changes, do not. If a child's freedom is not balanced by the brain's desire for imposed order, the child does less well as an individual and as a student.

A school dress code (or, better, the use of school uniforms) helps create an orderly learning environment. We recommend use of uniforms (even if just khaki slacks and buttoned white shirts) for all students. Uniforms help

to restore discipline and diminish peer pressure, help children to focus on learning rather than attire, and promote school unity.

As with single-sex classrooms and rites of passage, there is little downside to school uniforms. These innovations can help create the order the developing mind needs.

Other Innovations to Encourage Learning

➡ *Student-to-Teacher Ratio:* We recommend one teacher for every twenty students, although we know this is difficult for a larger school to attain.

Especially when the ratio is higher, teachers' aides and voluntary second teachers keep discipline problems lower and academic achievement higher.

➡ *Multigenerational Schools:* Having middle school and elementary school classrooms at the same location has, in the words of one teacher, "helped older kids stay younger and a little more innocent, in a good way, as well as helping them build compassion." The middle school kids are service-oriented and mentor-like toward the younger children. The younger ones enjoy the mentoring and role modeling of the older students and are encouraged to act more maturely.

➡ *Team Teaching:* A team of teachers meets every morning, for a few minutes. The members talk about troubled students, what lessons they have planned, how they can support one another, and how they can use a character lesson or the like from a colleague's class. As the team bonds, the students they teach are likely to feel themselves part of a community of teachers.

➡ *Single-Teacher Emphasis:* Some middle schools send students from classroom to classroom every hour. Research on the early-adolescent brain indicates a need for the presence of one teacher for the whole day, with other teachers coming in and out of the classroom to teach specialties. The homeroom teacher knows each student well and can nurture and mentor students as well as teach them. The teacher cannot shuttle a child with whom he or she is having problems to another classroom, so the teacher and student must work things out.

Students in middle school are in such personal upheaval that having one mentoring teacher creates a possibility for trust building, access to a caring adult when the student is in crisis, easy classroom management from the teacher's point of view, good discipline, and full opportunity for bonding and conflict-resolution activities throughout the day (which fits the early adolescent's diurnal rhythm well).

By the time puberty and cognitive developments are about completed (around age fifteen), the student is able to handle hourly movement from classroom to classroom.

➡ *Group Work and Pair Work:* Middle school students can benefit from increased group work and pair work.

High School

Many of the preceding structural innovations apply to high school. Additional innovations suggested for high school are as follows.

Class Size

The smaller the class size, the higher the potential for deep bonding with peers and teachers, and the lower the potential for discipline problems. Especially in early to middle adolescence, discipline is more easily accomplished if the student cannot hide in a big school or a big classroom. The seriously undisciplined student is often the bored and underachieving student who has decided to act out in order to call attention to his or her unstimulated brain. In smaller classrooms and schools, this student need not act out so severely to be noticed.

Classroom discipline is often dependent on everyone in the class being able to succeed at some moment. Especially during puberty (in which males must learn to manage themselves in the face of testosterone, the aggression and dominance hormone), boys are more likely than girls to show extreme acting-out behaviors and to drop out of class and school.

For boys, in particular, it's important to have one teacher for every twenty to twenty-five students, especially in classes that require a great deal of discussion (for example, English and social studies). Many boys feel inept at verbal skills in comparison to higher-alpha males and adept females. The lower the class size, the easier for these boys to compete and cooperate in the group.

For girls, it is especially important to reduce the size of classes that require high spatial and abstract skills (for example, physics). Lower-spatial girls often recede and lose personal power in an environment in which they feel less capable and are dominated by a few high-abstract girls and many high-abstract, loud boys. Smaller classes help these girls to find their voices and places.

Team Teaching and Homerooms

Whatever the class size, when teams of teachers are assigned to work with teams of students, the students feel the teachers' special interest in them and they get to know their teachers and other students within their teams very well. It is essential that students feel that they have a group to which they can relate at the high school level.

We suggest homerooms for all high schools, even through senior year. The brain learns best in a group or team that cares. In homerooms, students have opportunities to deal with academic and social issues through instruction and discussion. Homeroom classes should be small enough to allow all students to interact on more than a superficial level.

Use of School Time

➡ *Starting the School Day Later:* Brain research has focused on the relationship between teen sleep cycles and learning. Most high schools now start from 7:15 to 7:45 A.M. Most mid-teens need nine hours of sleep each night. Early starting times are cutting down on this sleep.

Michele Kipke, director of The National Academy of Science's Board of Children, Youth, and Families, says, "Sleep experts feel strongly that high school timings are out of sync with the natural circadian rhythms of adolescents." Our research corroborates this. Teachers say how difficult it is to teach teens in the early morning, especially in the already-tough teaching areas (verbal skills for many boys and higher math and physics for many girls).

William Dement, director of the Sleep Disorders Center of Stanford University, says, "Since the amount of sleep a student gets correlates strongly with academic performance and social behavior, it is important for high schools to have later start times."

Adolescents stay up later than they did earlier in life. The adolescent's circadian cycle is dominated by the need to learn management of personal energy—hormones and brain chemicals that are assaulting the system. Parts of the brain—especially in the limbic system and prefrontal areas—are experiencing accelerated growth that is natural to late evening. Forcing the adolescent to go to sleep is an unnatural solution. When schools start later, they find increased learning and fewer discipline problems.

➡ *Teaching Certain Subjects at Certain Times of Day:* Another innovation is in the timing of certain subjects during the school day. For instance, spatial learning is easier when the testosterone level is high, as at midmorning. This is a good time for math learning. Verbal learning can improve with estrogen increases. Although these are less diurnally cyclic than testosterone, teachers can note when girls' minds seem "electric" with learning; they may be perceiving estrogen surges in the girls' bodies. Band and art—which involve movement and whole-brain activity—should be taught early in the day, as they stimulate the sleepy brain by making demands on the body.

➡ *Extended School Hours and Saturday Classes:* Extending school hours and adding Saturday classes would help high schools to handle demands for more student learning and better use of students' leisure time. Saturday school and extended school hours especially should be considered for students with learning and/or behavioral problems. The more time the brain spends in learning and practicing its knowledge, the greater the chance of learning success.

Uniforms and Dress Codes

It is natural for adolescents to use clothing for individuation, attention, dominance, and mating strategies. Girls often dress provocatively, and boys often dress to reflect dominance. The more individualizing, competitive, and sexually oriented the culture, the more its adolescents use clothing, hairstyles, tattoos, jewelry, and other personal innovations to call attention to their growing sexual, social, and personal identities. They need limits to protect healthy development of the widest variety of brain systems.

High school should be a time of cooperative academic learning and maturity enhancement, not social competition, self-absorption, and sex. To the developing brain, learning and maturity are most important; any critical mass of other behaviors impedes the brain's ability to increase knowledge of social and academic skills that enhance success and personal maturity.

Before puberty, a great variety of stimulation (enhanced by focus) is the best brain food. As puberty hits, and as abstract cognitive development explodes in the developing brain (at about eleven to sixteen), the brain self-generates variety at an exponential rate and asks the culture to help it limit the variety that overwhelms development. Uniforms and other structural innovations that temper external psychosocial variety are immensely helpful to the adolescent brain.

We suggest at least a dress code for all schools. Generally, jeans, tee shirts, and gang or hip hop clothing are not allowed. Enforcement is firm; a first offense may entail a warning, a second offense may lead to a minor infraction notice, and a third offense can lead to a one-day suspension.

In schools where a dress code isn't enforceable without interruption in learning, uniforms may be the best option. Uniforms help to reduce male interruptive dominance behavior and female sexualized behavior. Students report that less provocative dress helps them to concentrate better on schoolwork. It also levels the field in terms of expense and trendiness in school clothing.

It is important to hold an assembly to explain the reasons for a clothing policy, as well as to promulgate it in homerooms and integrate it into discussions in classes such as social studies. Fitting it into character-education curricula is also helpful. In the end, students manage to adapt to the dress policy and often find it to be a new way of bonding and of representing the school.

Innovations Students Want

In a two-day student-teacher Mead Education Summit, hundreds of high school students brainstormed their most important requests of school systems. Students want what the brain wants for good learning:

- *Smaller class size.* This was at the top of the list. Students instinctively know their need for closer bonds and team learning environments.
- *More emphasis on technology.* With the competitive technological marketplace, high school students need more technological access and learning. High school is the perfect time to emphasize the influence of external technologies on the brain.
- *Support of AP and honors classes.* Students want greater options to increase learning at the highest levels, especially those that prepare them for college.

- *Focus on the arts.* Students felt that a great deal of emphasis went to sports and too little to band, choir, drama, photography, painting, and other arts. Both male and female students requested this, instinctively understanding the importance of these brain-expanding, interactive learning forms. Throughout K–12, boys want and need drama and other arts, including music. Schools can teach band in the morning rather than in the afternoon, when it might compete with athletic practice.
- *More field trips.* Both boys and girls wanted more field trips, especially for science learning. Planetariums, zoos, doctors' offices, government agencies—whatever the lesson, the students want to experience space-and-time stimulants that enhance it. Field trips are essential in helping girls who may not abstract scientific material as well as some males.

Alissa Sheehan conducted a survey of eleventh- and twelfth-grade students at Randolph, Massachusetts, High School. When asked what high school classroom activities stood out in their memories and what was important about these activities, the students responded as follows. Two females mentioned reading and editing, which girls tend to enjoy more than boys. The rest of the responses, from both males and females, described experiential and group activities, such as those described in this guide.

Female Responses

- Learning activities, playing games like "Who Wants To Be a Millionaire?" and "Spanish Bingo." In vocabulary, we drew pictures that would help us remember the vocabulary better. These activities brought fun to learning and helped me remember things.
- In several math classes, we went outside to actually apply what we were learning. In several different English classes, we acted out what we were reading.
- After reading *Macbeth,* we made a soundtrack with songs that had to do with different scenes. Something creative is always fun.
- Reading out loud, group activities, and just conversing with teachers.
- Peer editing; I understood how others were approaching activities we had for homework. By seeing how others do things, I gained ideas on how to do things in the future.

Male Responses

- Students had to make their own questions for a quiz to give to another group of students in the class.
- In tenth-grade history class, we learned about historical figures by making a dating game. In eleventh-grade math, we went outside and found the height of telephone poles using trigonometry.
- Reenacting historical events, such as the French Revolution. It helps you learn when you live it.
- Acting things out, group and individual work, videos, reenactments of past things, and role playing.
- Reenacting WWI on a giant map on the classroom floor in history class.
- We posed as leaders of countries at the Munich Conference and discussed our countries' points of view; this activity helps you understand what leaders of countries go through when making decisions for their countries.
- In ninth grade, after reading about Romeo and Juliet, our English teacher brought in fencing equipment to show us how they fought in the old days. It helped me get a hands-on experience about the book.
- Breaks (thirty seconds to one minute) in math class; it helps you relax.

When asked what activities teachers could do that would make them better students, both males and females again asked for the types of activities described in this guide.

Female Responses

- Games and fun associations. These help me concentrate better on the subject.
- More hands-on activities that involve more than just sitting in class and hearing lectures. Students learn better by doing things.
- The unexpected, like going outside to teach or forming teams and having group activities or brain teasers.
- More peer editing and revising.

Male Responses

- Things that show examples.
- I respond to visual aides; videos are fun. It is also fun to make trivia games based on the material being studied.

- Playing "Jeopardy" is a good way to review before a test because it is competitive and you learn about the subject as well. Also, more breaks throughout the period. I lose focus if the teacher does one thing for an hour or so.
- Field trips, going outside, puzzles, kidding around sometimes, acting things out, hands-on things, reading.
- Field trips and more group activities.
- Group work is a good learning technique.
- Activities that get you out of your seat and away from the books.
- More hands-on experience stuff.

Full Psychosocial Education

A sixteen-year-old boy said that he wished schools would teach things such as how to talk to girls, what they want from a guy, and so on. When asked about sex ed, the teen laughed, "That's kind of a joke." A girl said, "They teach you mostly things you know already or don't need, not what you really want to know." When asked, "Why do hardly any boys take the human growth and development classes?" a boy replied, "They're for girls, and women teach them." Both sexes complained about hurtful remarks and harassment from the other and about communication difficulties.

Parade magazine asked students "what life skills high schools should teach." Their responses were

- More about people of all cultures
- Social success skills
- Manners
- How to fix things
- Success theory—how to find a job
- How to protect yourself
- How to care for one another

Young people feel unaided in their psychosocial education. Their formal education about one another, which is perhaps one of the three most important things on their minds in high school (along with "Will I make it in life?" and "Who am I?"), is almost nonexistent.

IMPROVING SEX EDUCATION These days, the school is quite often the extended family. Many families are deficient in parenting teens (because of divorce, parent workload, or parenting style); most schools are coeducational; and the culture and media push males and females at one another in order to create the gender tension that sells products and movies.

Teenagers naturally take risks; it is the job of mentors and educators to help young people through their risk behaviors. The Centers for Disease Control and Prevention report that the only age group our culture has not been able to affect significantly with campaigns to reduce risky behavior is the statistical group from ten to twenty-four.

A recent national survey of adolescent males pointed out that television and school appear to be the primary sources of contraceptive information for young men; fewer than half receive information from their families. More than half of males age fifteen to nineteen have had intercourse. Until recently, sex-education support material emphasized female involvement more than male. *Involving Males in Preventing Teen Pregnancy: A Guide for Program Planners* by Freya Sonenstein and others makes the point that male involvement is not just about preventing pregnancy but also about helping young men become responsible husbands and fathers later in life.

Abstinence curricula are now part of sex education in many states. Alone, they are not enough to meet the needs of most sexually active teens, but they can be worthy additions to already existing programs, especially in late middle school and early high school. Most sex educators seek a middle ground between abstinence and contraception.

We suggest these innovations for sex education:

- Human growth and development classes should be team-taught, by a female teacher and a male (counselor, coach, teacher, father, or other volunteer).
- If a school is not going to make sex ed mandatory, parts of it should be taught in physical education and in other classes where boys are.
- Same-sex and separate-sex groupings both should be used, so that sensitive and difficult areas can be covered without members of either sex shutting down or resorting to attention-getting behaviors.

- In all sex education, fathers and other elder males should be conscripted to talk about a man's responsibilities and adolescent male feelings and experiences.
- Sex ed in some form should be taught in all years of high school, becoming more sophisticated and oriented to student questions as the students get older.

➡ *Parent training:* Anne de la Sota has added parent-training materials to sex ed packages, showing parents how to talk about it with teens.

GENDER EDUCATION Students want us to help them know what makes the other gender think and act as it does. Insights from brain-based research can be taught to students. Michael Gurian's books for boys (*From Boys to Men*) and girls (*Understanding Guys*) can help in this endeavor. High school students are mature enough to read Chapters One and Two of *Boys and Girls Learn Differently!* and to discuss the materials regarding brain-based gender differences and similarities.

➡ *Reviving the Wonder:* Ric Stuecker has cowritten a curriculum called *Reviving the Wonder,* which helps teachers and students facilitate dialogue between young males and females. He includes material from *Reviving Ophelia,* Mary Pipher's book on adolescent girls, and Michael Gurian's *The Wonder of Boys.* Ric recruits off-duty, retired, and other service-oriented adults to help mentor the gatherings of teenagers.

He and Suze Rutherford train adults in the kind of honest, compassionate gender dialogue they hope to create with young people. Then these adults help young people—in separate-sex and same-sex groups—prepare to communicate, have the dialogue, and process it. The program helps young people ask questions such as, "What is it about me as a woman (or man) that I want the other to know?" and "What are the things about the other I need to know?" The curriculum can be carried out by any counselor or teacher team, although it helps to receive the initial training or similar training in gender group dynamics. Ric and Suze also include asset-based training.

➡ *Teaching "Male Nature" to Boys:* Teachers should know enough about "male nature" to teach it to male students and help them gain insight into how to find personal worth and meaning in what they do.

➡ *Teaching "Female Nature" to Girls:* Girls also should be given training in the "female nature" to help them understand why they think and behave as they do and to help them find personal worth and meaning in what they do.

➡ *The Fishbowl Technique:* Young men sit in an outer circle; young women sit in an inner circle. Questions are asked and answered in the female circle, with the males silently observing. The circles are then switched, and the questions and issues are covered by the males, with the females silently observing. For many teenagers, this is a life-altering experience. If the adults join their gender groups and tell their stories along with the youths, it can be even more fruitful.

➡ *Question Lineups:* Another easy technique for dialogue is to have males on one side of the room and females on the other. Questions are asked and answered, first by one sex, then the other. After both groups have talked un-interrupted, they ask each other the deep questions. The leader facilitates mainly by making sure that silent youths have a chance to be heard, since a few dominant ones will do most of the talking.

➡ *Media Awareness:* Adolescents need to be taught about the effects of media imagery on male and female self-concepts and character development.

Some areas of specific concern for each gender cannot be handled by school systems unless the whole school, in many classes, embraces the importance of gender dialogue. Topics include

- Sexual harassment, which is a difficulty in any coeducational setting and a terrible problem in high-density, high-population high schools
- Gay bashing and lack of understanding of people who develop homosexually

- Sexual involvement, from flirting to intercourse, which is set up non-verbally in classrooms and other school areas even when it appears that students are focused on lessons
- The high extent to which young women feel they are disrespected, objectified, and dominated by male verbal and nonverbal communication
- The great extent to which young men feel overwhelmed by the relating styles of young women

Rites of Passage

Brain development and psychosocial maturity exist not only on an everyday continuum of experience but also in the context of "mini-crises" that are created by the brain's attention to its environment and by the community's attention to the brain. A child grows up by force of nature and environmental stimulants, but some of these stimulants need to be planned.

Perhaps the most lost service to teen development today is the rite of passage. We require our high school students to grow up by self-creating rituals, which take forms that may be high-risk and unnecessarily chaotic, from driving too fast to having sex for the first time. Unlike our ancestral cultures, we do not organize the adolescent journey into a set of mini-crises called rites of passage. Michael Gurian's books *The Good Son* and *A Fine Young Man* offer detailed structures for family-based, community-based, and school-based rites of passage.

At St. Mark's School in Texas, ninth-grade students go on the Pecos Wilderness Trip during the first two weeks of August each year. No student is allowed to be excused, except by certified medical waiver. The students, faculty, and community at St. Mark's consider this one of the most essential features of high school.

Near Los Angeles, the Millennium Oaks Institute holds a voluntary rite of passage in the fall of each year. Boys from thirteen to nineteen, along with fathers and mentors, engage in a series of half-day preparatory weekend gatherings that culminate in a retreat on a November weekend in the mountains. The three-month, rite-of-passage program focuses on self-expression, confidence, self-esteem, and leadership skill building.

These models and others like them are crucial to full development of the adolescent boy and girl. Without a rite of passage in which the community provides healthy crises to encourage psychosocial stimulation of the matura-tion process, certain areas of the brain (the prefrontal lobe and areas of the temporal lobe, which control moral and other psychosocial decision making) may not develop on schedule. This is especially true with high-risk youth.

Counterinnovations

Brain-based research tells us that we may have to throw out some practices that were once thought to be innovative.

STANDARDIZED TESTS Currently, high school males outscore females in standardized tests, by seven points in verbal areas and thirty-five points in math, although the males get 70 percent of the D's and F's in schools and only about 40 percent of the A's. Male adolescents naturally favor deductive and quick abstract reasoning and tend to quickly single out information rather than thinking out a larger variety of possibilities, so they tend to do well in a multiple-choice format. More males than females tend toward high risk taking and are likely to quickly answer questions under pressure and risk guesses. There is also an advantage for males in math testing because of the male-brain math advantage.

As standardized tests include more essay formats, even in math, females do better, bringing the male-female scores nearly to parity.

In June of 2002, the College Board announced that it would revise the SAT I to add a writing test that includes a handwritten essay, expand the math test to include topics from Algebra II while eliminating quantitative comparisons, and replace word-analogy questions with questions that assess reading comprehension. These changes were scheduled to appear in March of 2005.

GRADE INFLATION AND ACADEMIC FAILURE The brains of teenagers have trouble keeping up with everything we want them to learn. They require extra help—something teachers often cannot give. But they can inflate grades, which creates the illusion that the educational system is stable. As schools and students come under greater performance pressure, teachers in-flate grades in proportion to the pressures on the school system (for example, larger classes, students receiving less discipline, and standardized testing).

More boys than girls fail academically and more boys are the "beneficiaries" of grade inflation; this means that these boys are not getting the help they need. Although boys receive slightly higher scores on tests, they do not look as good statistically to colleges, which know about grade inflation in high school and the gender aspect of it.

Given that most college admissions officials give grades, class rank, and activities more weight than standardized test scores, high schools are challenged to deal with the various ways that male brains are not receiving the mentoring, challenge, bonding, direction, and academic education they need. Judith Kleinfeld completed one of the most comprehensive educational surveys and concluded that "males are more apt than females to believe that the school climate is hostile to them, that teachers do not expect as much from them and give them less encouragement to do their best."

The decline in male college admissions has become so serious that some officials are giving males a slight break. This is serious because college is a prime determinant of earning power and adult success.

APPENDIX: WORKING WITH PARENTS

Research shows the importance of collaboration between the home and school at every grade level. Parents should view teachers as an integral part of an extended family. The teacher's job is much easier if parents understand their children's developmental (emotional, mental, and physical) needs and work with teachers and schools to ensure the necessary bonding, discipline, and academic reinforcement that children need. Parent-school partnerships and school-based parent coordinators help to ensure this.

Preschool and Kindergarten

- Educate parents about brain-based gender differences in learning.
- Explain and stress the importance of bonding and familial support in a child's development and learning.
- Describe the desired class size and student-teacher ratio for maximum bonding and learning.
- Explain how parents can support the child's classroom development and learning.
- Ask parents to create daily reading rituals, reading to younger children and letting the child read to the parents.
- Ask parents to use math and spatial games at home.
- Explain the importance of good discipline at home, as well as daily rituals and routines.

Elementary School

- Ask parents to advocate structural innovations, such as year-round schooling, smaller schools, multigenerational classrooms, and a lower student-to-teacher ratio.
- Advocate teacher and parent training in gender-based brain and learning differences.
- Advise parents to get two or three professional opinions before putting a child on Ritalin, Prozac, or another psychotropic medication.
- Encourage parents to continue reading rituals in the home and to augment them with writing rituals (for example, making sure a child writes thank-you notes, birthday invitations, letters, and e-mails and keeps a journal).
- Encourage parents to instill character education in the home by example, by didactic instruction, and by spiritual storytelling.
- Work with parents to establish consistent discipline systems in the home, explaining the system the school uses and asking them to meld with that when possible.
- Teach parents brain-based techniques, such as giving a boy sixty seconds to fulfill a demand and giving a girl extra verbal encouragement.
- Encourage parents to stay in contact with teachers, volunteer for school activities, and become friends of the school.
- Encourage parents to plan their children's computer, television, and other technology use to best augment brain development.
- Help parents become more familiar with aggression nurturance and how it works, so they can guide it as well as empathy nurturance.
- Explain to parents the importance of being there (physically, emotionally, and conversationally) for their children.

Middle School

- Encourage parents to be very involved in their children's schooling, by attending parent-teacher conferences, volunteering, mentoring, and so forth.
- Ask parents to conduct rites of passage at home, within the extended family and its spiritual community, and with the school.

- Help parents to receive training in all aspects of adolescent biological development, especially brain and gender material, to aid their children's gender-based learning experiences.
- Encourage parents to teach empathy nurturance through example, didactic conversation, and storytelling.
- Help parents to learn about aggression nurturance and help direct it appropriately in early adolescents so as to increase strength, focus, attentiveness, and hierarchical success.
- Help parents to employ alternative strategies with those girls and boys who don't fit the gender types for their age groups or classes.
- Encourage parents to provide consistent discipline, especially regarding rewards and consequences for actions.
- Encourage parents to instill character development, in cooperation with the school's character program, and ask them to teach their children about social and sexual ethics.
- Help parents to understand the effects of prolonged exposure to video games and television on the developing adolescent brain.
- Help parents to develop, and ask them to consistently apply, media-time plans with early adolescent children.
- Ask parents to balance their children's sedentary (computer and study) activities with active (physical, sport, and athletic) ones so as to maximize brain development.
- Ask parents to monitor children's food intake (especially carbohydrates, sugars, and junk foods) carefully and to teach them the effects of diet on their physical and brain development.
- Encourage parents to spend more time with their young adolescents than the children seem to ask for, expecially in intergenerational pairs (mother-child time, father-child time, grandparent-child time, and so on).
- Ask parents to advocate smaller classrooms and separate-sex education in middle school.

High School

- Encourage parents not to give up their primary positions in their children's lives and to remain the most important supporting characters.

- Help parents learn to become active listeners and to ask their children important questions without judging the answers.
- Encourage parents to allow all topics of conversation, although rules of discourse (for example, "no cursing in front of younger siblings") can always apply.
- Ask parents to conduct extended-family rites of passage (sometimes connected to spiritual communities) and support school rite-of-passage experiences.
- Encourage parents to make older siblings partially responsible for the character education of younger ones (for example, if a film is inappropriate for a younger sibling, the teen does not view it in the younger one's presence).
- Encourage parents to give new freedom and responsibility to teens, in equal proportion (for example, with a new freedom, such as staying out past midnight, comes a new responsibility, such as a new set of chores).
- Ask parents to stress that homework and school activities are more important than leisure activities.
- Ask parents to instruct their children to treat all school personnel with respect, even when disagreeing with their policies or positions.
- Encourage parents to be involved with the school, through volunteering, attending activities, and school rite-of-passage experiences.

REFERENCES AND RESOURCES

Publications

Alvarado, A. "Professional Development *Is* the Job." *American Educator,* Winter, 1998.

American Association of University Women Educational Foundation. *How Schools Shortchange Girls: The AAUW Report.* Washington, D.C.: Author, 1992.

American Association of University Women Educational Foundation. *Gender Gaps: Where Schools Still Fail Our Children.* Washington, D.C.: Author, 1998.

American Association of University Women Educational Foundation. *Beyond the "Gender Wars."* (Originally presented at AAUW Educational Foundation Symposium, Sept. 2000.) Washington, D.C.: Author, 2001.

Arnot, R. *The Biology of Success.* New York: Little Brown, 2000.

Baker, R., and Bellis, M. *Human Sperm Competition.* London: Chapman and Hall, 1995.

Bear, M., Connors, B., and Paradiso, M. *Neuroscience: Exploring the Brain.* Baltimore, Md.: Williams and Wilkins, 1996.

Blake, J. "Fabulous Aunts . . . and Other Great Grown-ups: Adults Don't Have to Be Parents to Shape, Enrich a Youngster's Life." *The Seattle Times* (Northwest Life section), Feb. 3, 2002.

"Blueprint for Change: Report from the National Conference on the Revolution in Earth and Space Science Education." Report from the conference organized by the Center for Earth and Space Science Education at TERC, Cambridge, Mass., and the Center for Science, Mathematics, and Technology Education at Colorado State University, Fort Collins, Colo., May 16, 2002. Available online at www.EarthScienceEdRevolution.org; free print version available from communications@terc.edu.

Blum, D. *Sex on the Brain.* New York: Penguin, 1997.

Blythe, T. *The Teaching for Understanding Guide.* San Francisco: Jossey-Bass, 1999.

Borenson, H. *Hands-On Equations* (Program). Bloomington, Ind.: Phi Delta Kappa International, 1991.

Brandt, R. "Educators Need to Know About the Human Brain." *Phi Delta Kappan,* Nov. 1999.

Brody, J. "Kids Futures Could Be Weighed Down." *The San Diego Union-Tribune,* Apr. 22, 2002, p. D7.

Carton, B. "When Girls Wrestle Boys." *Wall Street Journal,* Jan. 19, 1999.

Dantonio, M. *Collegial Coaching: Inquiry into the Teaching Self* (2nd ed.). Bloomington, Ind.: Phi Delta Kappa International, 2001.

De Gaetano, G., and Bander, K. *Screen Smarts: A Family Guide to Media Literacy.* Boston, Mass.: Houghton Mifflin, 1996.

DeRoche, E. F., Sullivan, B. L., and Garrett, S. D. *Character Matters: Using Newspapers to Teach Character.* San Francisco: Use the News, 1999. (Also available through major newspapers.)

Diller, L. *Running on Ritalin.* New York: Bantam, 1999.

Fisher, H. *The Anatomy of Love.* New York: Fawcett Books/Ballantine, 1995.

Fried, S., and Weyforth, M. *On Target to Stop Bullying.* Kansas City, Mo.: Stop Violence Coalition, 1998.

Gardner, M. "State Bills Push Student Fitness." Copley News Service, Apr. 3, 2002.

Glenn, H. S., and Brock, M. L. *7 Strategies for Developing Capable Students.* Rocklin, Calif.: Prima, 1998.

Goldberg, B. *Bias: A CBS Insider Exposes How the Media Distort the News.* Washington, D.C.: Regnery Publishing, 2001.

Goleman, D. *Emotional Intelligence.* New York: Bantam, 1995.

Greene, J. F. *Language! A Literacy Intervention Curriculum* (2nd ed.). Longmont, Colo.: Sopris West, 2000.

Gurian, M. *The Wonder of Boys: What Parents, Mentors and Educators Can Do to Shape Boys into Exceptional Men.* New York: Tarcher/Putnam, 1996.

Gurian, M. *A Fine Young Man: What Parents, Mentors and Educators Can Do to Shape Adolescent Boys into Exceptional Men.* New York: Tarcher/Putnam, 1998. (Paperback, 1999).

Gurian, M. *From Boys to Men.* New York: Price Stern Sloan, 1999.

Gurian, M. *The Good Son: Shaping the Moral Development of Our Boys and Young Men.* New York: Tarcher/Putnam, 1999. (Paperback, 2000).

Gurian, M. *Understanding Guys: A Guidebook for Teen Girls.* New York: Price Stern Sloan, 1999.

Gurian, M. *Boys and Girls Learn Differently! A Guide for Teachers and Parents.* San Francisco: Jossey-Bass, 2001. (Paperback, 2002).

Gurian, M. *The Wonder of Girls: Understanding the Hidden Nature of Our Daughters.* New York: Pocket Books, 2002.

Gurian, M., and Trueman, T. *What Stories Does My Son Need? A Guide to Books and Movies That Build Character in Boys.* New York: Tarcher/Putnam, 2000.

Healy, J. *Failure to Connect: How Computers Affect Our Children's Minds and What We Can Do About It.* New York: Simon & Schuster, 1999.

Hennings, D.G. *Beyond the Read Aloud: Learning to Read Through Listening to and Reflecting on Literature.* Bloomington, Ind.: Phi Delta Kappa International, 1992.

Hoff Sommers, C. *Who Stole Feminism?* New York: Simon & Schuster, 1994. (Paperback, 1995, Carmichael, Calif.: Touchstone Books).

Hoff Sommers, C. *The War Against Boys: How Misguided Feminism Is Harming Our Young Men.* New York: Simon & Schuster, 2000. (Paperback, 2001, Carmichael, Calif: Touchstone Books).

Hoffman, H. A., Young, J., and Klesius, S. E. *Meaningful Movement for Children: A Developmental Theme Approach to Physical Education.* Needham Heights, Mass.: Allyn and Bacon, 1981. (Paperback, 1985, Dubuque, Iowa: Kendall/Hunt).

Hyerle, D. *A Field Guide to Using Visual Tools.* Lyme, N.H.: Designs for Thinking, 2000.

Jago, C. *With Rigor for All: Teaching the Classics to Contemporary Students.* Portland, Maine: Calendar Islands, 2000.

Jensen, E. *Teaching with the Brain in Mind.* Alexandria, Virg.: Association for Supervision and Curriculum Development, 1998.

Kandel, E., Schwartz, J., and Jessel, T. *Essentials of Neural Science and Behavior.* Norwalk, Conn.: Appleton and Lange, 1995.

Kleinfeld, J. "The Myth That Schools Shortchange Girls: Social Science in the Service of Deception." Fairbanks, Alaska: College of Liberal Arts, University of Alaska. www.uaf. edu/northern/schools/download.html

Koerner, B.I. "Where the Boys Are." *U.S. News and World Report,* Feb. 8, 1999.

Levine, M. D. *A Mind at a Time: America's Top Learning Expert Shows How Every Child Can Succeed.* New York: Simon & Schuster, 2002.

Manthey, J. "Boys and Girls Are Different! Creating Gender-Friendly Schools." Kid Culture in the Schools Workshop, Petaluma, Calif., 1998.

Manzo, T., and Manzo, U. *Teaching Children to Be Literate.* Orlando, Fla.: Harcourt Brace, 1995.

McNeil, L. "Creating New Inequalities." *American Educator,* June, 2002.

Meier, D. "Smaller Schools: More Smart Adults." *Los Angeles Times,* Aug. 1999.

Moir, A., and Jessel, D. *Brain Sex.* New York: Dell, 1990.

Moran, C. "Is Science Outrunning the Teachers?" *San Diego Union-Tribune,* Mar. 27, 2002, p. B1.

Neergaard, L. "Hospitalization of Overweight Children Is Rising Sharply." Associated Press, May 2, 2002.

Pert, C. *Emotion: Gatekeeper to Performance—The Mind/Body Connection* (Video). Bloomington, Ind.: Phi Delta Kappa International, 1999.

Phi Delta Kappa International. *Service Learning: Curriculum, Standards and the Community* (Video). Bloomington, Ind.: Author, 1991.

Pipher, M. *Reviving Ophelia: Saving the Selves of Adolescent Girls.* New York: Ballantine, 1995.

REACT, November 1–7, 1999. (Online magazine for teens published by JP Kids, Inc. www.react.com)

Reuters Health eLine. "TV Plus Meals Means Even More TV for Kids-U.S.," June 14, 2002; "Removing Bedroom TV May Cut Obesity Risk in Kids," June 3, 2002; "Rates of Childhood Obesity Rising Across Globe," May 28, 2002; "Obesity-Related Hospital Stays Rise Among U.S. Kids," May 1, 2002; "Doctors Warn of Rise in 'Couch Potato' Diabetes," Feb. 21, 2002; "Sugary Soft Drinks Linked to Childhood Obesity," Feb. 16, 2001; "Obese Children Have Unhealthy Arteries," Oct. 26, 2001; "Childhood Obesity a Growing Problem in U.S.," Oct. 13, 2000; "TV May Be Hazardous to a Child's Health," Sept. 26, 2000; "Parents Want Gym Classes Back in Schools," Sept. 12, 2000; "Lack of Exercise, Television Viewing Linked to Childhood Obesity," Mar. 25, 1998.

Ryan, K., and Bohlin, K. *Building Character in Schools.* San Francisco: Jossey-Bass, 1999.

Sadker, D., and Sadker, M. *Failing at Fairness: How Our Schools Cheat Girls.* New York: Touchstone, 1994.

Schmidt, M. *Smart Fats: How Dietary Fats and Oils Affect Mental, Physical, and Emotional Intelligence.* Berkeley, Calif.: North Atlantic Books, 1997.

Sheehan, A. L. Personal correspondence with Arlette C. Ballew. June 2002.

"Sleep Researchers Look to Changing School Hours." *The Washington Post,* Sept. 2, 1999.

Sonenstein, F. L., Stewart, K., Lindberg, L. D., Pernas, M., and Williams, S. *Involving Males in Preventing Teen Pregnancy: A Guide for Program Planners.* Washington, D.C.: The Urban Institute, 1998. www.urban.org/family/invmales.html

Stein, D. *Ritalin Is Not the Answer: A Drug-Free, Practical Program for Children Diagnosed with ADD or ADHD.* San Francisco: Jossey-Bass, 1999.

Stone, R. *Best Classroom Practices: What Award-Winning Elementary Teachers Do.* Bloomington, Ind.: Phi Delta Kappa International, 1999.

"Student Leaders Say Parents Vital to Success." Hearst Newspapers, Jan. 28, 1999.

Stuecker, R., and Rutherford, S. *Reviving the Wonder: 76 Activities That Touch the Inner Spirit of Youth.* Champaign, Ill.: Research Press, 2001.

Sugar, S., and Sugar, K. K. *Primary Games: Experiential Learning Activities for Teaching Children K-8.* San Francisco: Jossey-Bass, 2002.

Sullivan, A. "Why Do Men Act the Way They Do?" *Reader's Digest,* Sept. 2000.

Sylwester, R. *A Celebration of Neurons: An Educator's Guide to the Human Brain.* Alexandria, Virg.: Association for Supervision and Curriculum Development, 1995.

Taylor, S. E., Klein, L. C., Lewis, B. P., Gruenewald, T. L., Gurung, R.A.R., and Updegraff, J. A. "Biobehavioral Responses to Stress in Females: Tend-and-Befriend, Not Fight-or-Flight." *Psychological Review,* July 2000, *107* (3).

U.S. Department of Education. *National Education Assessments.* Washington, D.C.: Author. (Various years).

Van Bronkhorst, E. "Grade Inflation Rampant." Associated Press, Mar. 29, 1998.

Will, G. "Drugs Not Good for What Ails Them." *The Washington Post,* Dec. 7, 1999.

Wiske, M. S. (ed.). *Teaching for Understanding: Linking Research with Practice.* San Francisco: Jossey-Bass, 1998.

Wolfe, P. *Brain Matters: Translating Research into Classroom Practice.* Alexandria, Virg.: Association for Supervision and Curriculum Development, 2001.

Organizations, Programs, and Services

Act-React®, c/o G.H. Weedman, 607 Tumbleweed Court, Kokomo, IN 46901. Phones: 765-459-4778, 941-768-1250. www.cyberroad.com/act-react

American Association of University Women Educational Foundation, 1111 Sixteenth Street N.W., Washington, D.C. 20036. Phones: 202-728-7602, 800-326-2289; Faxes: 202-463-7269, 202-872-1425. www.aauw.org and foundation@aauw.org

Association for Supervision and Curriculum Development, 1703 North Beauregard Street, Alexandria, VA 22311-1714. Phones: 703-578-9600, 800-933-ASCD; Fax: 703-575-5400. www.ascd.org

Big Brothers Big Sisters of America, 230 N. 13th Street, Philadelphia, PA 19107. Phone: 215-567-7000; Fax: 215-567-0394. www.bbbs.org

Capabilities, Inc., c/o H. Stephen Glenn, PMB 438; 2305-C Ashland Street, Ashland, OR 97520. Phones: 541-552-1475, 800-222-1494. www.capabilitiesinc.com

The College Board, 45 Columbus Avenue, New York, NY 10023-6992. Phone: 212-713-8000. www.collegeboard.com

Designs for Thinking, 144 Goose Pond Road, Lyme, NH 03768. Phone/Fax: 603-795-2757. designs.thinking@valley.net

Fast ForWord™, c/o Scientific Learning™, 300 Frank H. Ogawa Plaza, Suite 500, Oakland, CA 94612-2040. Phone: 888-665-9707; Fax: 510-444-3580. www.fastforward.com

Gender and Education Association (*Gender and Education* journal), c/o Carfax Publishing/ Taylor & Francis (UK). North American Customer Service Center: 7625 Empire Drive, Florence, KY 41042. Phone: 800-634-7064; Fax: 800-248-4724. www.taylorandfrancis. inetapress.com

The Graphic Organizer (Greg Freeman). www.graphic.org

ICA Rite of Passage Journeys, Institute of Cultural Affairs in the USA, 22401 39th Avenue S.E., Bothell, WA 98021. Phone: 425-486-5164. www.icajourneys.org or www.ica-usa.org

Innovative Learning Group (Thinking Maps®). 1011 Schaub Drive, Suite 200, Raleigh, NC 27606. Phones: 919-233-7188, 800-243-7169; Fax: 919-233-6695. www.thinkingmaps.com

Lindamood-Bell™, c/o Nancibell Inc./Gander Educational Publishing. Phones: 805-541-5523, 800-554-1819.

The Michael Gurian Institute. www.gurianinstitute.com or www.michael-gurian.com

National Training Associates, P.O. Box 1270, Sebastopol, CA 95472. Phone: 800-624-1120; Fax: 707-874-0129. www.nta-yes.com

The National Urban League, Inc., 120 Wall Street, New York, NY 10005. Phone: 212-558-5300; Fax: 212-344-5332. www.nul.org

The Parent Institute, P.O. Box 7474, Fairfax Station, VA 22039-7474. Phones: 703-323-9170, 800-756-5525; Faxes: 703-323-9173, 800-216-3667. custsvc@parent-institute.com

Parents as Teachers National Center, Inc., 2228 Ball Drive, St. Louis, MO 63146. Phones: 314-432-4330, 866-728-4968; Fax: 314-432-8963. www.patnc.org

Phi Delta Kappa International, P.O. Box 789; 408 N. Union Street, Bloomington, IN 47402-0789. Phones: 812-339-1156, 800-766-1156; Fax: 812-339-0018. www.pdkintl.org

Rite of Passage, 1561 Highway 395, Minden, NV 89423.

S.C.O.R.E. (Schools of California Online Resources for Education). www.score.k12.ca.us

Stop Violence Coalition, 301 E. Armour, Suite 440, Kansas City, MO 64111. Phone: 816-753-8002.

The Teacher Institute, P.O. Box 397, Fairfax Station, VA 22039-0397. Phones: 703-503-5413, 800-333-0776; Faxes: 703-323-9173, 800-216-3667. custsvc@teacher-institute.com

Teaching Tolerance, c/o Southern Poverty Law Center, 400 Washington Avenue, Montgomery, AL 36104. Phone: 334-956-8200. www.splcenter.org/teachingtolerance/tt-index.html

TERC, 2067 Massachusetts Avenue, Cambridge, MA 02140. Phone: 617-547-0430; Fax: 617-349-3535. www.terc.edu

U.S. Department of Education, 400 Maryland Avenue S.W., Washington, DC 20202-0498. Phone: 800-872-5327. www.ed.gov

U.S. Department of Education, Office for Civil Rights. www.ed.gov/offices/OCR.

Washington State Safe Schools Coalition, c/o NWCHD, P.O. Box 21428, Seattle, WA 98111-3428. Phone: 206-632-0662, ext. 49 (messages). www.safeschoolscoalition.org

Youth Leadership Development Intensive, c/o The Scherer Yeoell Group, 421 W. Riverside Avenue, Suite 1000, Spokane, WA 99201. Phones: 509-838-8167, 800-727-9115; Fax: 509-623-2511. www.sygroupinc.com

THE AUTHORS

Michael Gurian is an educator, family therapist, and author of three national best-sellers, including *The Wonder of Boys,* which has been published in ten foreign languages. *Boys and Girls Learn Differently!* was his fourteenth book. He is cofounder of the Michael Gurian Institute (www.gurianinstitute.com), where teachers are trained in brain-based and gender innovations. He is an international lecturer whose work has been featured in *The New York Times, The Wall Street Journal, USA Today, The Washington Post, Time, Newsweek,* and other major print media, as well as on the "Today Show," "Good Morning America," PBS, and CNN. He lives in Spokane, Washington, with his wife, Gail, a family therapist, and their two children. He can be reached at www.michaelgurian.com.

Arlette C. Ballew is a writer and editor who specializes in experiential learning, training, education, and human resource development. She is the coauthor of the seven volumes of Pfeiffer & Company's *Training Technologies Series* and of *Earthquake Survival: Activities and Leader's Guide*; the coeditor of the four volumes of *Theories and Models in Applied Behavioral Science*; and the developer of many experiential training activities, educational and training packages, leader's guides, and workbooks. She lives in San Diego, California.

THE GURIAN INSTITUTE

THE MICHAEL GURIAN INSTITUTE IS A LEARNING ENVIRONMENT IN WHICH TEACHERS, from preschool through high school, apply the best of the new science in their everyday classrooms and share results with other teachers. These teachers have been trained in how boys and girls learn differently and have developed innovations to fit their new knowledge.

The teachers in the two-year Gurian Institute pilot program in Missouri helped develop the blueprint for the "ultimate classroom" that appears in *Boys and Girls Learn Differently!* The blueprint has already had success in their schools and school districts (for example, in the Hickman Mills School District in Kansas City, discipline problems were cut by 35 percent within six months of teacher training in how boys and girls learn differently).

The St. Joseph, Missouri, school district focused the Gurian Institute training on one school, Edison Elementary, headed by Principal Debbie Murphy. This elementary school had consistently tested at the lowest ends of the academic spectrum. Ms. Murphy applied a number of core training models, culminating in an immersion of her key staff in the Gurian Institute in the 1999–2000 school year. As a result of this training, Edison students tested in the top five (of eighteen) slots in their school district, sometimes in first and second. Statewide, Edison outscored state data in every subject area, sometimes doubling or tripling the number of students in the top achievement levels. Out of four hundred students, only two required state-mandated retesting. There also was a dramatic decline in discipline problems.

The Gurian Institute training in the specific learning styles of boys and girls, and in gender-specific teacher-, student-, and parent-bonding strategies, helps educators to fully educate all their students. It has changed the way many schools go about the business of education.

The Michael Gurian Institute now provides training internationally. The Gurian Institute staff is committed not only to training teachers and parents but also to making participant school districts, corporations, and agencies self-sufficient in their ability to train their own staffs in ongoing ways.

If you would like to bring the information and innovations in this publication to your community, please contact the Gurian Institute for more information (www.gurianinstitute.com).

INDEX